Love from
Nazanin Nalini
xxxxx ♡

Kazu

alex Gardner
thanks
for
teaching me

Ella

Masaru Aoki
...♡♡MASSY♡♡...
.....♡MASSO♡......

Ben
Sorry
you
are
leaving.

Arash kamvar.

Dumbard

Erica
good luck

Ally Hull

Nicky
Band

Monde
☺

Richard →

Claire Kreisky

Love

Good Luck

SHILLA

Zoe S,

Jean-Paul   Juki Cameron   Ochi

Good
luck from
Natasha
xxx

Love Anne
(Virgnal!)

Nelemir   Loaba   Etan

Sarah Wybrow.
Rleko uchinaka ♡
Julia kalache
Pooneh sanai

Sophia Hoite.
Jamie kay
Tam pollard
Masaki   Zayed
Daniel Schutzman.
Iris Ferber

Joseph   Daryl   Love Benjamin I hop you
ABBEY   Have a Nice hav a nice time. X X B
Ellie Barda time.
Tomoaku
Oliver Daly   GOOD
Gary   LUCK Laura
                RYUICHI XXXX
BenJamin   ASAI
Sohail
Ida   Hooman Belania
MITA ♡♡♡
XXXXXX X   To,
Sarah
XX++T   Anna,
Katharine
XXXXXXXXXXXX   I am Sad you are
Iona   leaving, have a pleasent
Helen Martyn   future
XXXX   M Keller
                   M. Keller

Very best wishes for the future / Teresa

Best Best Wishes for the coming year, Please come back! Louise

Wish every Good. Wishes & Many thanks — John & Evan Tyrrell Wilson.

To Anna Radons

from

Paragon Hill School

Hampstead

Enjoy yourself and hope to see you back. Love Quita +

dear Anna, lots of luck & best wishes for your future. happiness, you're a hard act to follow!!! love & many thanks. Pauline xxx

Anna All the best of luck. Love one ...

July 1588

To Anna Radons

I hope you have a good Time from Simon

Very much love & gratitude Ralph

BONNE CHANCE Bernard

Writers and Hampstead

Writers and Hampstead

Observations on the Place and the People
101 Commentators from Domesday to Drabble

·

Chosen and Edited by
IAN NORRIE

·

Calligraphy by
GEORGE SIMPSON

·

Architectural Photographs by
KEITH WYNN

High Hill Press, Hampstead,
1987

First published by the High Hill Press,
6a Hampstead High Street, London, NW31PH in 1987

ISBN: 0 900462 23X

Printed by Butler and Tanner Limited,
Selwood Printing Works, Frome, Somerset

Contents

Please leave this
page.
(for photo and staff names)

INTRODUCTION:

Countless scribes have had their say about Hampstead. Here are highlighted just 101 of them, but the number could be 1001 because although not every writer has found a permanent home in N.W.3, many more than have lived here have commented upon the place. It is a subject which arouses deep emotions. Most of those quoted are on its side; some are not. The selection is personal. Distinguished writers, living and dead, are omitted, many reluctantly, some with relief. I would like to have included John Galsworthy who was a resident in Admiral's Walk for fifteen years but could find no reference in his works. Stella Gibbons was a strong candidate with her novel "Here Be Dragons," yet I could not find a short extract which pleased me. Anyone else's selection would be different though not totally so because who could have left out Keats, Leigh Hunt, Dickens....Alan Coren? I wish there could have been some Shakespeare, but if there were we surely would have heard by now?

This book is based on the exhibition mounted at Burgh House, New End, in March/April 1986 as part of the Hampstead Millennium celebrations. There are a few additions, and more deletions (mostly illustrations), and the order and categories of the exhibition have not always been retained; the calligraphy, much praised when exhibited at Burgh House, has.

IAN NORRIE, July, 1986

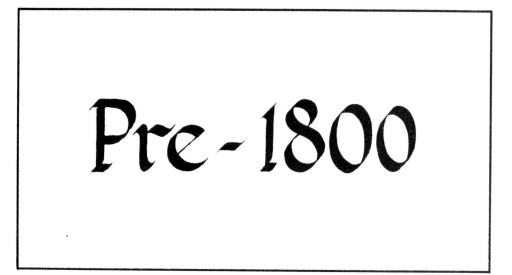

Pre - 1800

John Evelyn

Opposite: *Fenton House, Hampstead Grove.*
Recent resident custodians were Richard Usborne,
author of works on P.G. Wodehouse, and Anne, his wife,
whose drawings adorn "Portrait of Hampstead."

9

THE·DOMESDAY·BOOK

HAMPSTEAD'S·FIRST·MENTION·IN·A·BOOK RESULTED·FROM·THE·DOMESDAY·SURVEY OF·1086.

> ⓂＨ*AMESTEDE* teñ abͫ Ѕ *PERI*. ɪɪɪɪ. hid. Ṫra. ɪɪɪ.
> car. Ad dñiū ptiñ. ɪɪɪ. hid 7 dim. 7 ibi. ē. ɪ. car. Viłłi
> hñt. ɪ. car. 7 alia poṫ fieri. Ibi. ɪ. uiłł de. ɪ. uirg. 7 v.
> bord de. ɪ. uirg. 7 ɪ. feruͦ. Silua. c. porc. Iñ totū
> uał. ʟ. fol. Qͩdo recep. fimił. T.R.E. ⸍c. fol.
> Ｉn ead uiłła teñ Rañ peurel fub abͫe. ɪ. hidā
> de ṫra uiłłoᵹ. Ṫra dim car. 7 ibi eft. Ħ ṫra ualuit
> 7 uał. v. folid. Hoc Ⓜ totū fimul jacuit 7 jacet in dñio
> æcclæ Ѕ *PETRI*. *IN SPELETORNE HVND.*

TRANSLATED·INTO·MODERN·ENGLISH·THIS MEANS·THAT THE ABBOT OF ST. PETER'S (WESTMINSTER) OWNS HAMPSTEAD AND 3½ OF THE 4 HIDES BELONG TO HIM. THERE IS LAND FOR 3 PLOUGHS OF WHICH THE VILLAGERS HAVE ONE. 1 VILLAGE HAS ONE VIRGATE (ABOUT 30 ACRES); 5 SMALLHOLDERS SHARE ONE. THERE IS ONE SLAVE. IN THE WOODLAND 100 PIGS. THE TOTAL VALUE IS 50 SHILLINGS AND WAS THE SAME WHEN IT WAS ACQUIRED, WHICH WAS BEFORE 1066.

IN THE SAME VILLAGE RANULF PEVEREL HAS 1 HIDE OF GROUND UNDER THE ABBOT AND LAND FOR ½ PLOUGH. THE VALUE OF THIS LAND IS 5s.

THE WHOLE MANOR IS AND WAS UNDER THE LORDSHIP OF ST. PETER'S CHURCH.

MICHAEL DRAYTON (1563-1631)

But Hampstead pleads, himself in simples to have skill,
And therefore by desert to be the noblest hill;
And challengeth, from them, the worthiest place her own
Since that Old Watling once, o'er him to pass was known.

from "Poly-Olbion," c. 1598

SAMUEL PEPYS (1633-1703)

Secretary to the Admiralty, diarist, in his own lifetime were published his <u>"Memoirs of the Navy."</u> There are two references to Hampstead - both consistently spelt or misspelt - in the <u>"Diary."</u>

THE LADY NOT THE PLACE

.... and thence had Mary meet me at the New Exchange, and there took coach and I with great pleasure took the ayre at Highgate and thence to Hamsted. Much pleased with her company, pretty and innocent....

from "Diary" 11/12 July, 1665

ORANGES AND LEMONS IN BELSIZE

Up and by water to White-hall, and so to St. James's; and thence with Mr. Wren by appointment in his coach to Hamsted, to speak with the Atturny general, whom we met in the fields by his old route and house. And after a little talk about our business of Ackeworth, went and saw the Lord Wotton's house and garden, which is wonderful fine; too good for the house, the gardens are; being endeed the most noble that ever I saw – and rare Orange and lemon trees.

from "Diary" 15/17 August, 1668

[The Attorney General was Sir Geoffrey Palmer.
Lord Wotton owned Belsize House.]

13

JOHN EVELYN (1620-1706)

Diarist and traveller, author of works on arboriculture, engraving and smoke pollution.

TEARS OF CLAY

We returned in the evening by Hampstead to see Lord Wotton's house and garden – Bellsize House – built with vast expense by Mr. O'Neale, an Irish gentleman who married Lord Wotton's mother. The furniture is very particular for Indian cabinets, porcelain and other solid and noble moveables. The gallery very fine, the gardens very large, but ill-kept, yet worthy and changeable. The soil a cold weeping clay not answering the expense.

from "Diary," June 2, 1676

14

SIR RICHARD STEELE (1672-1729)

Dramatist, politician and essayist, best known for his contributions to "The Spectator." Member of the Kit-Cat Club which met in Hampstead in summer months. Sedley, 1639-1701 was a wit and playwright.

'I am at a solitude, an house between Hampstead and London, wherein Sir Charles Sedley died. This circumstance set me a-thinking and ruminating on the employments in which men of wit exercise themselves.'

Letter to Alexander Pope, June 1, 1712

[Sedley died in poverty; Steele was at the house – later painted by Constable – to evade his creditors.]

DANIEL DEFOE (1660-1731)

Immensely prolific author, satirist, traveller, creator of "<u>Robinson Crusoe</u>" and "<u>Moll Flanders,</u>" and, for some years, also a secret agent. His journeys did not overlook Hampstead.

M.V. der Gucht Sculp.

Laudatur et Alget
Juven. Sat. I.

PROPERTY SPECULATION ALREADY RIFE

Hampstead indeed is risen from a little country village, to a city, not upon the credit only of the waters, though 'tis apparent, its growing greatness began there; but company increasing gradually, the people liking both the place and the diversions together; it grew suddenly populous, and the concourse of people was incredible. This consequently raised the rate of lodgings, and that increased buildings, till the town grew up from a little village, to a magnitude equal to some cities; nor could the uneven surface, inconvenient for building, uncompact, and unpleasant, check the humour of the town, for even on the very steep of the hill, where there's no walking twenty yards together, without tugging up a hill, or straddling down a hill, yet 'tis all one, the buildings increased to that degree, that the town almost spreads the whole side of the hill.

NO JOGGERS THEN

On the top of the hill indeed, there is a very pleasant plain, called the Heath, which on the very summit, is a plain of about a mile every way and in good weather 'tis pleasant airing upon it, and some of the streets are extended so far, as that they begin to build, even on the highest part of the hill. But it must be confessed, 'tis so near heaven that I dare not say it can be a proper situation, for any but a race of mountaineers, whose lungs have been used to a rarefied air, nearer the second region, than any ground for 30 miles round it.

from "Tour through the Whole Island of Great Britain", 1724-6

17

SAMUEL JOHNSON (1709-1784)

Lexicographer, poet, man of letters wrote the first seventy lines of his most famous poem in a single day of 1748 while visiting his wife, Tetty, at Priory Lodge, on the corner of Frognal and Branch Hill. The house was demolished in the 1920s.

18

COMPLEMENTARY

The needy traveller, serene and gay,
Walks the wild heath, and sings his toils away.
Does envy seize thee? Crush th'upbraiding joy,
Increase his riches and his peace destroy;
Now fears in dire vicissitude invade,
The rustling brake alarms, and quiv'ring shade,
Nor light nor darkness bring his pain relief,
One shews the plunder, and one hides the thief.

Lines 36-44 from "The Vanity of Human Wishes."

'One man can learn more in a journey
by the Hampstead coach than another
can in making the grand tour of Europe.'

Quoted in "Streets of Hampstead," 1984

FANNY BURNEY (1752-1840)

Novelist, daughter of the musical historian, Charles Burney and wife of General d'Arblay, with whom she was interned by Napoleon. She was a frequent visitor to Hampstead during the second period when the Wells became fashionable.

THE LONG AND SHORT OF IT

The ball was at the long room at Hampstead.

This room seems very well named, for I believe it would be difficult to find any other epithet which might, with propriety, distinguish it, as it is without ornament, elegance, or any sort of singularity, and merely to be marked by its length.

from "Evelina", Volume 2, Letter 19, 1778

ANNA LAETITIA BARBAULD (1743-1824)

Wife of a minister of the Rosslyn Hill Chapel who lived at 8, Church Row with her niece, Lucy Aikin. Edited "The British Novelists" in 50 volumes and wrote many books for children.

WEST END FAIR

And now away for West End Fair
Where whisky, chariot, coach and chair
 Are all in requisition.
In neat attire the Graces
Behind the counters take their places,
 And humbly do petition
To dress the booths with flowers and sweets,
 As fine as any May-day,
Where charity and fashion meets
 And keeps her play-day.

from "The Hampstead Garner," ed. A.M.C. (1906)

EDWARD COXE

Lived at Heath End House, and was neighbour of Lord Erskine, the Lord Chancellor, whom he successfully prevented from felling the nine elms of the poem. They endured until 1876.

UNPOLLUTED VIEW

It is a goodly sight through the clear air
    From Hampstead's healthy height, to see at once
    England's vast capital in fair expanse
Towers, belfries, lengthened streets and structures fair.

from "London".

22

The 19th Century

John Keats

Leigh Hunt

LUCY AIKIN (1781-1864)

Author of Memoirs of the Courts of Elizabeth I, James I, Charles I, and a life of Joseph Addison, she lived at 8, Church Row around 1800. She was the niece of Mrs. Barbauld.

AN EARLY NINETEENTH CENTURY VIEW

Several circumstances render society here peculiarly easy and pleasant. In many respects the place unites the advantages and escapes the evils both of London and provincial towns. It is near enough to allow its inhabitants to partake in the society, the amusements, and the accommodations of the capital as freely as ever the dissipated could desire; whilst it affords pure air, lovely scenery, and retired and beautiful walks. Because everyone here is supposed to have a London set of friends, neighbours do not think it necessary, as in the provinces, to force their acquaintance upon you; of local society you may have as much, little, or none, as you please; and with a little, which is very good, you may associate on the easiest terms. Then the summer brings an influx of Londoners, who are often genteel and agreeable people, and pleasingly vary the scene. Such is Hampstead.

from a letter to the Rev. Dr. Channing, of Boston, quoted in several histories.

24

JOANNA BAILLIE (1762-1851)

Dramatist and poet, Scottish by birth, lived at Bolton House, Windmill Hill, from 1791 until her death. Sir Walter Scott visited her there. Her plays were performed at Drury Lane, Sarah Siddons appearing in at least one of them.

The Muses, since the birth of Time,
Have ever dwelt on heights sublime.
On Pindus now they gather'd flowers,
Now sported in Parnassian bowers;
    And late, when Murray deign'd to rove
    Beneath Caen Wood's sequester'd grove,
    They wander'd oft, when all was still,
    With him and Pope on Hampstead Hill.
One eve as they inhal'd the breeze,
They mark'd a little clump of trees,
And chose it for their fav'rite shrine;
The Trees were Elms – the number Nine.

from "Miscellaneous Poetry," 1805

LEIGH HUNT (1784-1859)

Poet, essayist, editor of "The Examiner," printed Keats' first poem. Was jailed for his outspoken comments about the Prince Regent but continued to edit his paper from prison. Wrote five sonnets to Hampstead. Lived first in West Hampstead, later in the Vale of Health, probably in Vale Lodge but also in a cottage since demolished.

A CONFINEMENT OF POETS

.... Our little packing-case – dignified with the name of house.... I defy you to have lived in a smaller cottage than I have done. Yet it has held Shelley and Keats and half a dozen friends in it at once; and they have made worlds of their own within the rooms....

Quoted by Barratt in "Annals," Volume Two

28

A steeple issuing from a leafy rise,
With farmy fields in front and sloping green,
Dear Hampstead, is thy southern face serene,
Silently smiling on approaching eyes,
Within, thine ever-shifting looks surprise,
Streets, hills and dells, trees overhead now seen,
Now down below, with smoking roofs between, –
A village, revelling in varieties.
Then northward what a range, – with heath and pond
Nature's own ground; woods that let mansions through,
And cottaged vales with billowy fields beyond,
And clump of darkening pines, and prospects blue,
And that clear path through all, where daily meet
Cool cheeks, and brilliant eyes, and morn-elastic feet.

Written after Hunt's release from jail in 1815.

Vale Lodge

JOHN KEATS (1795-1821)

Hampstead's most distinguished poet lived at
Wentworth Place, Albion Grove (now Keats Grove)
from 1818-20, having previously lodged in Well Walk,
with his brother Tom.

PLACES OF NESTLING GREEN FOR POETS MADE

I stood tip-toe upon a little hill,
The air was cooling and so very still
That the sweet buds which with a modest pride
Pull droopingly, in slanting curve aside,
Their scantly leaved and finely tapering stems,
Had not yet lost those starry diadems
Caught from the early sobbing of the morn.
The clouds were pure and white as flocks new shorn,
And fresh from the clear brook; sweetly they slept
On the blue fields of heaven, and then there crept
A little noiseless noise amongst the leaves,
Born of the very sigh that silence heaves,
For not the faintest motion could be seen
Of all the shades that slanted o'er the green.

from "The Story of Rimini," 1817

Said by Gittings, and other Keatsian authorities to refer to
Hampstead Heath, the brook could have been the then
unenclosed Fleet River.

ENCOUNTER ON NEW YEAR'S EVE

.... I thoughtlessly gave you a promise for Sunday - now I have just received a 'yes' from a friend of mine to pass that said day here - so be lenient and your petitioner shall ever pray &c. I met Wordsworth on Hampstead Heath this morning....

from a <u>Letter</u> to Benjamin Robert Haydon, written from Hampstead on 31.12.1817

MY DEAR BROTHER AND SISTER....

Within this last week I have been every where - and I will tell you as nearly as possible how all go on - with Dilke and Brown I am quite thick - with Brown indeed I am going to domesticate - that is we shall keep house together - I shall have the front parlour and he the back one....

.... Poor Kirkman left wentworth place one evening about ha' past eight and was stopped, beaten and robbed of his Watch in Pond Street....

.... Mrs. Brawne who took Brown's house for the Summer, still resides in Hampstead - she is a very nice woman - and her daughter senior is beautiful and elegant, graceful, silly, fashionable and strange - we have a little tiff now and then....

from a <u>Letter</u> to the George Keatses, 16.12.1818 - 4.1.1819

Dilke and Brown were co-owners of Wentworth Place, Kirkman was a visitor from Portsmouth, 'daughter senior' was, of course, Fanny.

THOMAS HARDY (1840-1928)

Novelist, poet, epic dramatist. His only recorded Hampstead connection is the poem he wrote after visiting Keats House.

AT A HOUSE IN HAMPSTEAD.
SOMETIME THE DWELLING OF JOHN KEATS.

O Poet, come you haunting here
Where streets have stolen up all around
And never a nightingale pours one
    Full-throated sound?

Drawn from your drowse by the Seven famed Hills
Thought you to find all just the same
Here shining, as in hours of old,
    If you but came?

What will you do in your surprise
At seeing that changes wrought in Rome
Are wrought yet more on the misty slope
    One time your home?

Will you wake wind-wafts on these stairs?
Swing the doors open noisily?
Show as an umbraged ghost beside
    Your ancient tree?

Or will you, softening, the while
You further and yet further look,
Learn that a laggard few would fain
    Preserve your work?....

Where the Piazza steps incline
And catch late night at eventide,
I once stood in that Rome and thought,
    " 'Twas here he died."

I drew to a violet-sprinkled spot
Where day & night a pyramid keeps
Uplifted its white hand, & said
    " 'Tis here he sleeps."

Pleasanter now it is to hold
That here, where sang he, more of him
Remains than where he, tuneless, cold,
    Passed to the dim.

July, 1920

ROBERT LOUIS STEVENSON (1850-1894)

Author of "Treasure Island," "Kidnapped," "A Child's Garden of Verses," etc. In 1874 he stayed at Abernethy House, Mount Vernon.

Hampstead is the most delightful place for air and scenery near London. I cannot understand how the air is so good, it does not explain itself to me; coming up out of London is like going to the top of Kirk Yetton. I have been out here all day, walking and strolling about the heath.

from a letter to a friend in Scotland.

WILLIAM BLAKE (1757-1827)

Poet, artist, visionary. He disliked North London in general and in particular Hampstead where he visited his friend the painter John Linnell at Collins' Farm.

A journey to Hampstead without due consideration would be a mental rebellion against the Holy Spirit, and only fit for a soldier of Satan to perform.

Quoted by Barratt in "The Annals"

KATE GREENAWAY (1846-1901)

Foremost creator of books for children in late Victorian times, as author and artist. Came to live at 39, Frognal, in a house designed by Norman Shaw, in 1885. Died there in 1901

ELYSIAN FROGNAL

I believe you're thinking I'm not finding Hampstead to my mind – but that is very far from the case. If you'd ever lived in Pemberton Gardens – you'd know what a comfort this house must be to me and if you had lived in Holloway you would know – what sort of a paradise Hampstead must seem.

from a Letter to Norman Shaw, 29.4.1885, quoted in Rodney Engen's "Kate Greenaway," 1981

36

JOHN RUSKIN (1819-1900)

Art historian, first Slade Professor of Art at Oxford University.

WHAT'S IN A NAME?

"You're not going to call your house a villa! Could you call it Kate's State – or Kitty's Green – or Brownie's Cell – or Camomile Court – or Lassie's Leisure – or the Romp's Rest – or – something of that sort?"

from a letter to Kate Greenaway who was about to move into 39, Frognal, 1885

38

ELIZABETH BARRETT-BROWNING (1806-1861)

LETTER TO R.B.

Dearest, I have been driving out before your letter came.... and to *Hampstead!* think of that. And see the proof of it – this grew in the hedges when the sun rose today. We had a great branch gathered, and 'this was of it!' starred over with dog-roses....

Monday Morning, (postmark June 9, 1846)

ROBERT BROWNING (1812-1889)

LETTER TO E.B.B.

....While I write this, my lips rest on the eglantine....well, it shall be 'dog-rose' for Flushie's sake. .....A rose from Hampstead! And you bore the journey well? You should tell me, precisely, detailedly.

Tuesday (postmark June 9, 1846)

[*Flush, Elizabeth's dog, had recently bitten Browning.*]

from "Letters of Robert Browning and Elizabeth Barrett-Browning, 1845/6," pub. 1899

WILKIE COLLINS (1824~1889)

Novelist, friend of Dickens, son of landscape painter William Collins, R.A. Author of "The Moonstone," "The Woman in White," etc., long supposed to have lived in Church Row but modern researchers can find no evidence for this.

WALTER HARTRIGHT'S WALK IN HAMPSTEAD
31 July – 1 August, 1849

[*Walter Hartright, an impecunious drawing master, and hero of*
Wilkie Collins's "The Woman in White," begins his story with a visit to his
mother's cottage in Hampstead, where he had walked from his 'chambers'
off the Strand. The cottage was at the very top of the village, near
Jack Straw's Castle — Lower Terrace perhaps, or Heath Brow.]

It was one of the two evenings in every week which I was accustomed to spend with my mother and sister. So I turned my steps northward, in the direction of Hampstead.... The quiet twilight was still trembling on the topmost ridges of the Heath; and the view of London below me had sunk into a black gulf in the shadow of the cloudy night when I stood before the gate of my mother's cottage....

[*He had taken the most direct route, through Holborn and Camden Town to*
South End Green and up the East Heath. Over the meal he learned from a
fellow-guest, the Italian political exile Pesca, about the offer of a job as drawing
master at a stately home in Cumberland, which was to involve him in the great
adventure of his life: an adventure which was to start sooner than he expected.
He left full of excitement about his new prospects —]

It was nearly midnight when the servant locked the garden-gate behind me. I walked forward a few paces on the shortest way back to London; then stopped and hesitated–

The moon was full and broad in the dark blue, starless sky; and the broken ground of the Heath looked wild enough in the mysterious light, to be hundreds of miles away from the great city that lay beneath it. The idea of descending any sooner than I could help into the heat and gloom of London repelled me.... I determined to stroll home in the purer air, by the most roundabout way I could take; to follow the white winding paths across the lonely Heath; and to approach London through its most open suburb by striking into the Finchley Road, and so getting back, in the cool of the new morning, by the Western side of the Regent's Park....

I wound my way slowly over the Heath [*he was probably following the line of what is now Oak Hill Way*] enjoying the divine stillness of the scene, and admiring the soft alternations of the light and shade as they followed each other on the broken ground on every side of me... [*He now descended into what is now Frognal Lane and*] ....arrived at that particular point of my walk where four roads met – the road to Hampstead, along which I had ret- urned; the road to Finchley; the road to West End [*i.e. West End Lane*]; and the road back to London. I had mechanically turned in this latter direction, and was strolling along the lonely high-road – idly wondering, I remember, what the Cumberland young ladies would look like [*he must have been approaching what is now the corner of Arkwright Road*] – when, in one moment, every drop of blood in my body was brought to a stop by the touch of a hand laid lightly and suddenly on my shoulder from behind me.

I turned on the instant, with my fingers tightening round the handle of my stick.

There, in the middle of the broad, bright high-road – there as if it had at that moment sprung out of the earth or dropped from the heaven – stood the figure of a solitary Woman, dressed from head to foot in white....

CHARLES DICKENS (1812-1870)

Dickens was never resident in Hampstead although following the death of his sister-in-law in 1837 he stayed for a while at Collins' (now Wyldes) farmhouse at North End. He was also a regular visitor to both the home of his friend Clarkson Stanfield in the High Street and to Jack Straw's Castle. There are many references to Hampstead in his novels and letters.

THE FLIGHT OF SIKES

He went through Islington; strode up the hill at Highgate on which stands the stone in honour of Whittington; turned down to Highgate Hill, unsteady of purpose, and uncertain where to go; struck off to the right again, almost as soon as he began to descend it; and taking the foot-path across the fields, skirted Caen Wood, and so came out on Hampstead Heath. Traversing the hollow by the Vale of Health, he mounted the opposite bank, and crossing the road which joins the villages of Hampstead and Highgate, made along the remaining portion of the heath to the fields at North End, in one of which he laid himself down under a hedge and slept.

Soon he was up again, and away, – not far into the country, but back towards London by the high-road – then back again – then over another part of the same ground as he had already traversed – then wandering up and down in fields, and lying on ditches' brinks to rest, and starting up to make for some other spot, and do the same, and ramble on again.

from "Oliver Twist," Chapter 48

TRANSACTIONS OF THE PICKWICK CLUB

May 12, 1827. Joseph Smiggers, Esq., P.V.P.M.P.C.*, presiding. The following resolutions unanimously agreed to:—

'That this Association has heard read, with feelings of unmingled satisfaction, and unqualified approval, the paper communicated by Samuel Pickwick, Esq., G.C.M.P.C.*, entitled "Speculations on the Source of the Hampstead Ponds, with some Observations on the Theory of Tittlebats;" and that this Association does hereby return its warmest thanks to the said Samuel Pickwick, Esq., G.C.M.P.C., for the same.'

from "Pickwick Papers", Chapter 1

> * Perpetual Vice-President — Member Pickwick Club
> * General Chairman — Member Pickwick Club

KENWOOD SAVED!

'The scouts reported further, that this party meeting with some others who had been at similar work (rioting and arson) elsewhere, they all united into one, and drafting off a few men with the killed and wounded, marched away to Lord Mansfield's country seat at Caen Wood, between Hampstead and Highgate; bent upon destroying that house likewise, and lighting up a great fire there, which from that height should be seen all over London. But in this, they were disappointed, for a party of horse having arrived before them, they retreated faster than they went, and came straight back to town.'

from "Barnaby Rudge," Chapter 66

Kenwood House

INVITATION TO JACK STRAW'S

'You don't feel disposed, do you, to muffle yourself up, and start off with me for a good brisk walk over Hampstead-heath? I knows a good 'ouse there where we can have a red-hot chop for dinner, and a glass of good wine....'

from a Letter to John Forster, his biographer, 1838

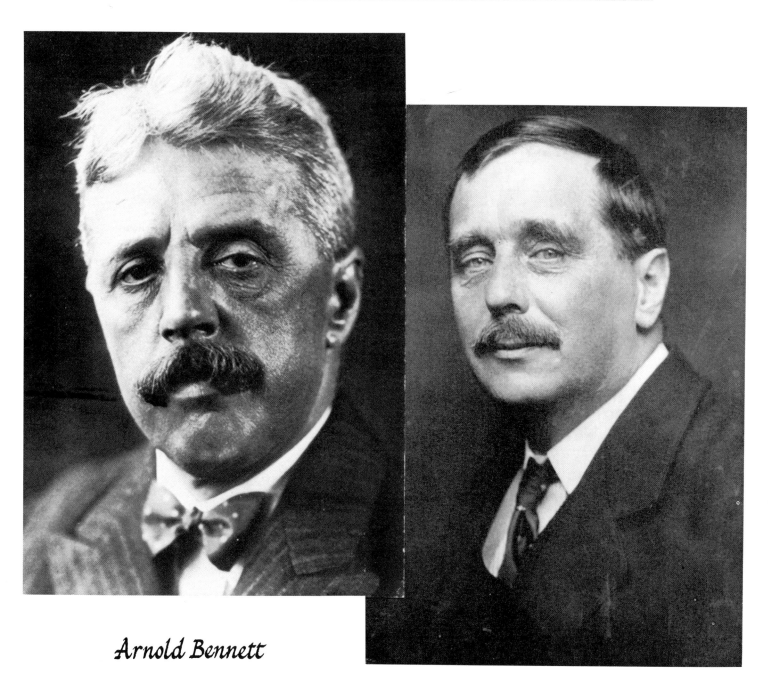

Late Victorian and Edwardian

Arnold Bennett

H. G. Wells

ARNOLD BENNETT (1867-1931)

Novelist – "The Old Wives Tale," "Anna of the Five Towns," "Clayhanger," "Imperial Palace," etc. – immensely prolific writer, journal, letters, reviews. Knew everyone in the literary world.

AT 17, CHURCH ROW

Tuesday, 21 December – Dined at <u>Wells's</u>, Lowes Dickinson, the Rothensteins and T. Seccombe. Rothenstein a good talker. Richard Whiteing, Mrs. Nevinson, and a whole family of Radfords came in after. The whole family was exceedingly typical. The worn bright mother, the pure, downright, clever daughters, all young, and the elegantish young son. Also a doctor who could do excellent Cockney imitations....

Thursday, 23 December – To lunch at <u>Wells's</u>. He and I talked his scandal from 12.15 to lunch-time....

from "<u>The Journals</u>," 1909

H. G. WELLS (1866-1946)

Novelist, historian, vicarious spaceman, womaniser. His earliest association was with West Hampstead where he taught at Henley House School, Mortimer Crescent, Kilburn, the Principal of which was J.V. Milne, Christopher Robin's grandfather. A pupil in the 1870s was the future Lord Northcliffe.

THE PRESS AT POOH CORNER

Somewhen about the age of twelve, Master Harmsworth became possessed of a jelly-graph for the reproduction of MS. in violet ink, and with this he set himself to produce a mock newspaper. J.V. with the soundest pedagogic instinct, seized upon the educational possibilities of this display of interest and encouraged young Harmsworth, violet with copying ink and not quite sure whether he had done well or ill, to persist with the "Henley House Magazine" even at the cost of his school work. The first number appeared in 1878; ..... During my stay at Henley House, I contributed largely, and among others who had a hand in the magazine was A.J. Montefiore, who was later to edit the "Educational Review" and A.A. Milne ("aged six" — at his first appearance in print) the novelist, essayist and playwright.

from "*Experiment in Autobiography*," 1934

> The 'jellygraph' was given to young Harmsworth by George Jealous, proprietor of the 'Ham & High, a neighbour in the Vale of Health.

50

DAVID GARNETT (1892-1981)

Author of "Lady into Fox," etc., and three volumes of autobiography. One of the Bloomsbury group, his second wife was Angelica Bell. Son of Edward and Constance Garnett, attended University College School but before it moved to Hampstead.

GAMES AUTHORS PLAYED

I only went once or twice to tea with the Wellses and remember being rather flabbergasted at the energy and noise H.G. put into some of the games he made us play. There was rampageous bumping round a table and knocking over of chairs when I had expected to sit around, on my good behaviour, listening to highbrow conversation. And then I was dragged into a nursery where a little war was in progress and saw H.G., in a whirlwind of tactical enthusiasm, ousting his small sons Frank and Gyp from the peaceful enjoyment of their toy soldiers.

I don't think Wells took much notice of me then: but a year or two later, meeting me by the Hampstead Fire Station, opposite the Tube, he said, "You are following exactly in my footsteps and I suppose later on you'll throw up biology to write novels".

from "The Golden Echo," 1970

JEANNE MACKENZIE (1922-86) and NORMAN MACKENZIE (1921-)

Jointly biographers of Dickens, Wells and "The First Fabians," individually, authors of works on diverse subjects. Lived in Hampstead at three different addresses between 1945-64. Norman became a member of the first faculty of the University of Sussex.

WELLS IN AND OUT OF CHURCH ROW

H.G., who had never intended to establish himself in a town house, was distinctly uncomfortable in 17, Church Row. When he had acquired it, he had had it in mind to go away with Amber. When he had to live in this pleasant Georgian terrace, he found himself saddled with a house which was much less spacious than his Sandgate house, more difficult to run, and unsuitable for the kind of entertaining he enjoyed.

He certainly liked the fact that he could stroll out on to Hampstead Heath, or go for longer walks into the country with Haynes and other friends who shared his taste for a good tramp. It was agreeable to have old friends living near by. The Radfords had moved to Hampstead. So had the Garnetts, who had taken a house in Downshire Hill, and the Rothensteins were round the corner in Oak Hill Park. And Hampstead was near enough to town for people to come out for lunch or dinner, or to parties where the customary games and charades were carried on as energetically as ever.

from "The Time Traveller," 1973

[17, Church Row was the Wells family house from 1909-12 but for part of that time H.G. was absent, having eloped with Amber Reeves.

52

BEATRICE WEBB (1858-1943)

Social reformer, early Fabian, married to Sidney Webb (Lord Passfield), founder of "The New Statesman". They lived at 10, Netherhall Gardens from November 1892- October 1893, shortly after their marriage.

AUSTERITY WITHIN THE WEB

Gloomy November weather finds us settled three hundred feet above the sea in a cosy little flat in South Hampstead. Our life an even tenor of happiness. In the last two months engaged on indexing and arranging our material....and writing a brief skeleton of the first volume of our book. Each morning we begin work about 9·30 (breakfast and reading papers and letters take an hour). Galton joins us about ten and we three drive through material until one or one thirty. Then Sidney hurries off to London and gives the remainder of his day to the London County Council.... I spend a couple of hours either walking on the Heath or travelling to London on shopping errands. At 4 o'clock Galton and I have a cup of tea and a chat and again set to work until 6 or 6·30. At 7·30 Sidney returns full of the doings of the L.C.C., of carrying back news of an interview with a cabinet minister on some proposed reform. A simple meat supper, cigarettes, and then an evening of peaceful happiness, either him reading to me, or working on L.C.C. matters, or we entertain working-men friends and so forth. Dinner-parties we have resolutely eschewed, I finding that I cannot keep a clear brain for work with talk exciting the evening.

from "Diary of Beatrice Webb," December 1892

[The book was their "History of Trade Unionism"; Galton was their secretary.]

MARGARET OLIVIER (1859~1943)

Wife of Sydney, Baron Olivier, who was Secretary of the Fabian Society, 1886~9, Governor of Jamaica, 1907~13, Secretary for India, 1924 and uncle to Laurence Olivier.

ANARCHY ~ HAMPSTEAD-STYLE

The "Hampstead Historic" meetings at the time I began to go to them were to a certain extent presided over by Mrs. Charlotte Wilson and were held at her home in a cottage on Hampstead Heath called Wildwood Farm. Arthur Wilson, her husband, kept in the background, but Mrs. Wilson, who called herself an Anarchist, was a clever speaker besides being a kind and gracious hostess. She seemed to me a very peaceful sort of Anarchist, so did all the others who came to the meetings, some of them Russians. Mrs. Dryhurst, who also called herself an Anarchist, came and with her the young lady who afterwards became Mrs. Edward R. Pease. There were also the Fabian Socialists, <u>Webb</u>, Wallas, <u>Shaw</u>, and others. Someone read a paper and this was followed by discussion, often very vigorous and exciting and lasting till Mrs. Wilson interrupted it with sandwiches and drinks, after which we all turned out on to the Heath.

from "Sydney Olivier: Life and Letters," 1948

Wylde's →

GEORGE BERNARD SHAW (1856-1950)

Dramatist, critic, vestryman of St. Pancras. Many of his plays were performed at the Everyman Theatre in the 1920s. The world premiere of "Cymbeline Refinished" was at the Embassy Theatre, Swiss Cottage, on 16.11.1937. He was never a resident of, but often visited, Hampstead.

HAMPSTEAD REFERENCES IN SHAW'S PLAYS

"In the name of common decency, Harry, will you remember that you are a gentleman, and not a coster on Hampstead Heath on Bank Holiday?"

Cokane to Trench in "*Widowers' Houses*", 1892

"I had rather go and live in some cheap place like Bedford Square or even Hampstead than take a farthing of his money."

Stephen Undershaft to his mother in "*Major Barbara*", 1905

The study windows, which have broad comfortable window seats, overlook Hampstead Heath towards London. Consequently, it being a fine afternoon in spring, the room is sunny.

Stage directions in "*Back to Methuselah*", 1921

"I went up to town on an invitation from some artistic friends in Fitzjohn's Avenue...."

Vivie to Praed in "*Mrs. Warren's Profession*", 1898

MICHAEL HOLROYD (1935–)

Biographer of <u>Lytton Strachey</u>, who did live in Hampstead, and of <u>Bernard Shaw</u>, who did not. He is married to <u>Margaret Drabble</u>.

SCHOLAR

FABIANS AT WYLDES

In the late 1880s Shaw joined a political group that started as the Karl Marx Club and developed into the Hampstead Historic Society, which met fortnightly at Wyldes' Farmhouse, North End which belonged to a stockbroker, Arthur Wilson. At the centre of the discussion group was his wife Charlotte Wilson, a firebrand from Newnham College, Cambridge, who kept chickens and created an idealised kitchen that owed much to her hero William Morris, but where no cooking took place.

The Hampstead Historic Society became the chief policy making forum of the Fabians. Shaw, Sidney Webb and the other Fabians would stride to and from Hampstead arguing so outspokenly that other socialists, and especially other socialists' wives, could not believe they would remain friends. Once indoors, Mrs. Wilson would read out "Das Kapital" in French "until" Shaw explained "we began to quarrel...."

Subsequently Charlotte persuaded the club to turn from Marx to Proudhon and her farmhouse was later invaded by strange foreign gentlemen such as a Russian nihilist who had fled from St. Petersburg after stabbing to death the chief of the Russian secret police, and who was to die caught by the heel ("Achilles-like" Shaw suggested) on a suburban level-crossing.

Shaw owned shares in the Hampstead Garden Suburb for many years. He also contributed to the "Ham & High": on "Socialism in Hampstead" (5.11.1887); on a concert of the Musical Guild in the Hampstead studio of Henry Holiday (1.2.1890); and on the subject of "Lord Mansfield's Fence" in a letter of 13.7.1901. He also lectured for the Hampstead Ethical Institute at the Hampstead Conservatoire on 13.11.1919 on "Modern Religion".

In 1920 Norman Macdermott founded the Everyman Theatre (now cinema) and re-introduced Shaw's plays to London. To help him Shaw gave a lecture at the Hampstead Town Hall.

Condensed from notes supplied by Michael Holroyd, 1985

GEORGE DU MAURIER (1834-1896)

Novelist and artist. Had four Hampstead addresses, Gangmoor, Whitestone Lane, Holly Mount, Church Row and New Grove House. Father of Gerald du Maurier.

FACTION

She had never seen Hampstead Heath, which I knew by heart; and Hampstead Heath at any time, but especially on a sunny morning in late October, is not to be disdained by any one.

Half the leaves have fallen, so that one can see the fading glory of those that remain; yellow and brown and pale and hectic red, shining like golden guineas and bright copper coins against the rich, dark, business-like green of the trees that mean to flourish all the winter through, like the tall slanting pines near the Spaniards, and the old cedar-trees, and hedges of yew and holly, for which the Hampstead gardens are famous.

from "Peter Ibbetson," 1896

Gangmoor

New Grove House

SIR GERALD DU MAURIER (1873-1934)

Actor manager, especially associated with the plays of J. M. Barrie. Son of George du Maurier, father of Daphne du Maurier. Born at 27, Church Row, lived at Cannon Hall from 1916 until death.

TRILBY was written at New Grove House, Hampstead, where my father and all of us lived for about twenty years. I have the desk still on which all the drawings were made, and the chair in which he sat whilst he drew them and all his other pictures for PUNCH. His output was phenomenal for a man with one eye, and that eye a very frail one, upon which livelihood depended. He had the strange faculty of being able to work, that is to say write and sketch, in a studio where people wandered in and out, chatted, played and sang at the piano, where dogs barked to be taken out for a walk, and where a canary would perch on his pencil whilst he was concentrating his attention on a child's profile and at the same time planning out the next chapter of the novel he was writing.

from the Preface to "Trilby" in the Everyman Edition, 1931

DAPHNE DU MAURIER, D.B.E. (1907-)

Novelist, dramatist, author of "__Rebecca__," "__Jamaica Inn__," etc., daughter of actor __Gerald du Maurier__ (who was born at 27, Church Row) and grand-daughter of novelist and "Punch" cartoonist, __George du Maurier__.

CANNON HALL

I soon discovered that our lavatory window led on to a flat roof over the dustbins in the courtyard, and by climbing out of this window, and creeping along this same flat roof, one could drop down over the dustbins and reach the courtyard. This was promptly discouraged. A pity. It damped adventure.

The garden at the back of the house made up for this disappointment. First a lawn, then, encircled by bushes, a parapet that looked down on to the lower garden several feet below, where there was a herbaceous border, and also vegetables. I would walk along the narrow parapet, eyes front, while Jeanne, below me in the lower garden, would try to climb up through it unseen, and so surprise me. This she seldom achieved.... There were also the coal-shed and the woodshed, which in days gone by had been the old Hampstead lock-up. So now we had a real prison – when the gardener was at his vegetables – to transform into a cell, its blackened walls and barred slit windows daunting to whichever of us was taking the part of prisoner at the time.

from "__Growing Pains__," 1977

Jeanne was her sister. The family had recently moved from Cumberland Terrace. The lock-up is still there, on Cannon Lane.

64

SIR STANLEY UNWIN (1884-1968)

Distinguished publisher who lived much of his life in Hampstead, for the last fifty years in Oak Hill Park.

A PUBLISHER IS NEVER OFF DUTY

Just over four months after the start of George Allen and Unwin, [1914] my wife and I were married on my birthday at Lyndhurst Road Congregational Church, Hampstead, by Dr. R. F. Horton. In the vestry afterwards I had laughingly said to him, 'You ought to write your autobiography.' To my joy he did so.

from "The Truth about a Publisher," 1960

Between the Wars

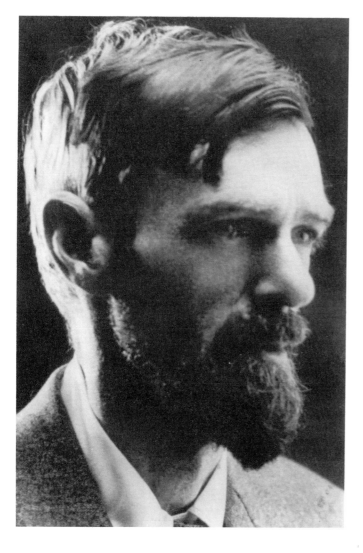

D. H. Lawrence

Catherine Carswell

CATHERINE CARSWELL (1879-1946)

Novelist who lived in Holly Bush House, Holly Mount for many years. Married to Donald Carswell, barrister, who checked D.H.Lawrence's "Women in Love" for libel. Also lived, amongst other NW3 addresses, at 110, Heath Street.

MESSIAH IN HEATH STREET?

Arrived at Hampstead the problem was how to get Lawrence up to the first floor. Kot and Murry had to carry him. But in their enthusiasm they went on with their burden, up and up, until their brother, asleep on the top storey, was awakened by the trampling, stumbling sound, and ran out in alarm to the little landing. He told me afterwards that when he saw clearly before him St. John and St. Peter (or maybe St. Thomas) bearing between them the limp figure of their master, he could hardly believe he was not dreaming.

from "The Savage Pilgrim" 1931

NOSTALGIA RULES

I lived in old Hampstead, mostly in charming old houses near the Heath, for about twenty-eight years. I might have grown old there – all passion spent – a gentle Hampstead old age, notwithstanding public and personal disasters. Others have done so. I sometimes go up to see them in the well-loved little streets.

But Hampstead is all reminiscence, beautifully and tenderly preserved as it were under a glass case. The Heath often looks like an old, well-tended tapestry. Perhaps it was this preserved, exclusive exquisiteness that put Lawrence into a resentful rage against Hampstead, when for a time he lived there. He could not fit his flaming life into its nostalgic scene, nor rejoice in moving, himself so painfully alive, in a souvenir.

from "Lying Awake" 1950

D. H. LAWRENCE (1885-1930)

Novelist, poet, dramatist, painter, etc., lived, as briefly as he lived anywhere, at 1, Byron Villas, Vale of Health, in 1915; at 32, Well Walk, in 1917; at No. 1, Elm Row, in 1923; and at 30, Willoughby Road, in 1926. He also stayed with the Carswells at 110, Heath Street in the winter of 1923/4. Frieda (von Richtofen) eloped with Lawrence from 40, Well Walk in 1912.

There was a little snow on the ground, and the church clock had just struck midnight. Hampstead in the night of winter for once was looking pretty, with clear white earth and lamps for moon, and dark sky above the lamps.

A confused little sound of voices, a gleam of hidden yellow light. And then the garden door of a tall, dark Georgian house suddenly opened, and three people emerged. A girl in a dark blue coat and fur turban, very erect: a fellow with a little despatch-case, slouching: a thin man with a red beard, bare-headed, peering out of the gateway down the hill that swung in a curve towards London.

"Look at it! A new world!" cried the man in the beard as he stood on the step and peered out.

"No, Lorenzo! It's only whitewash!" cried the young man in the overcoat.

from "The Last Laugh," a short story, 1924

John Carswell says the scene 'is undoubtedly the garden gate of 110, Heath Street.' The two men are Lawrence and Middleton Murry; the girl is Dorothy Brett.

70

JOHN MIDDLETON MURRY (1889-1957)

Journalist, critic, biographer, married to Katherine Mansfield, 1918-1923. After her death he lived for a while in the 1920s at 1a, The Gables, Vale of Health.

.... On a beautiful afternoon in late July 1914 Campbell, Katherine and I with the Lawrences took the tube for Hampstead. All went well until we reached the Hampstead Station. We emerged in good order, and began to advance up the steep road immediately opposite Holly Bush Hill. We three hung back a little, so that the Lawrences were well ahead. Suddenly, there was a piercing cry of 'Lawrence!' and we had a hasty glimpse of a young lady, clad it seemed in a kimono, rushing with enthusiastic arms outspread down the hill. 'Good God!' said Campbell. 'I won't have *that*!' said Katherine. With one accord we sped down the hill, round the corner and fled. The lady from whom we fled in such panic discourtesy is now Madame Litvinov.

When he returned home Lawrence was very angry.... we had made him look a fool. He had turned round to introduce us, and we just weren't there.

from "Between Two Worlds", 1935

[*Madame Litvinov was the English novelist who married the Bolshevik emissary to the Court of St. James.*]

72

The Gables, Vale of Health

KATHERINE MANSFIELD (1888-1923)

New Zealand born shortstory writer and poet, who was married to John Middleton Murry in 1918. From then until the autumn of 1920 they lived at No. 17, East Heath Road.

A GREY WORLD

I did not want what the poor middle-class want – and I have grey nearly everywhere. All the doors are to be grey, and the skirting boards, &c and shutters, with black stair banisters and black treads. In the kitchen, white distemper with turquoise blue paint. On the top floor your room – lemon yellow with grey cupboard. The bathroom real canary yellow – and the external paint for the railings, gate and door, grey again.

from a letter to LM (her friend Ida Baker), June 1918

E. M. FORSTER (1879-1970)

Novelist and man of letters, there are no explicit local connections, but in "A Passage to India", 1924, Dr. Aziz, when told that Fielding is returning to England, says

'I suppose you will visit Miss Quested.'

'If I have time. It will be strange seeing her in Hampstead.'

'What is Hampstead?'

'An artistic and thoughtful little suburb of London —'

VIRGINIA WOOLF (1882-1941)

Novelist, diarist, wife of Leonard Woolf.
Did not live in Hampstead, did not like Hampstead.

ENEMY TERRITORY

So the question for me is, how far to withdraw from unsympathetic society in the future? Is this cowardly or merely good sense? For instance, here is Brett already inviting us into the heart of the enemies camp — Hampstead Thursday evenings. If I go I shall be rasped all over, or at any rate dulled & blunted....if I don't go shall I soften & rot in the too mild atmosphere of my own familiars?

from "Diary", Tuesday, 22nd August, 1922

77

LYTTON STRACHEY (1880-1932)

Biographer of "Eminent Victorians," "Queen Victoria," "Elizabeth and Essex," one of the Bloomsbury Group. Lived first at 67, Belsize Park Gardens, later at No 6. Appeared at the Old Hampstead Town Hall at tribunals to register his conscientious objection to fighting in world war one.

THE FIRST HOUSE IN BELSIZE PARK GARDENS

There is a basement billiard-room, the darkest chamber I've ever seen in my life, and without a billiard table. Your mother, mine and I found ourselves locked into it, and thought we'd be discovered three crumbling skeletons – forty years hence. Fortunately I was able to leap a wall and attract a caretaker.

from a letter to Duncan Grant, 1907, quoted in Michael Holroyd's "Lytton Strachey," 1967

SIR STEPHEN SPENDER (1909 –)

Poet, editor of "Horizon," 1939/41, co-editor, "Encounter," 1953-67, friend of Auden and Isherwood. Educated at University College School, Frognal in which road he also lived in the 'twenties.

INTRODUCTION TO 10, FROGNAL

Caroline noted that it was an ugly house in the Hampstead style, as if built from the box of bricks of a nineteenth-century German child. It was surmounted by an abortive tower at one corner, to vary the regularity of the roof. There was a stone-tiled hall, long and high, out of which doors led to a dining-room containing massive furniture, and to Harold Spender's book-lined study, which had a roll-top desk. Upstairs was a drawing-room, painted grey, and furnished in a style reminiscent of Mrs. Spender's *art nouveau* phase. Above this there was a floor which contained several bedrooms.

from "World Within World," 1951

[Caroline Alington went to live with the young Spenders after the death of their mother.]

80

FIREMAN SPENDER

I was moved to a station at Maresfield Gardens in Hampstead. As I now lived next door to the station it was often possible to escape home. Thus I got more of my work done than at the sub-station. This station was distinguished by the presence of several remarkable men: amongst them William Sansom, the writer, who had arranged for me to be transferred there; Fernando Henriques, a Jamaican of vitality and considerable intelligence; and one or two musicians from London orchestras. The Officer-in-charge, like many London firemen, an old sea-dog, both bluff and sly, giving the impression of roaring round the station all day long, but really exercising a good deal of diplomacy. He treated me with tolerance.

from "World Within World," 1951

[Spender joined the Auxiliary Fire Service in 1942.]

University College School

ELEANOR FARJEON (1881-1965)

Author of "A Nursery in the Nineties," of many children's books, poems and of plays in collaboration with her brother Herbert. Lived at 20, Perrin's Walk from 1920 until her death.

NO. 23 THE HIGH

Everybody who lived in Hampstead between the two World Wars knew Mrs. Pyett's antique shop in the High Street. It stood below Barclays Bank, the Health Food Stores, and the old fashioned jeweller's in whose window queer clocks of other days performed their tricks. A metal poodle with a dial embedded in his flank lolled his tongue in and out with the passing seconds. Modernity surged in with a plate-glass display of motor-cars, succeeded by mortality in the Funeral Furnishers, whose window-show consisted of three caskets, between which on Sundays two large dormant cats advertised the pleasures of eternal rest. And then you were arrested by the exciting window of No. 23 (*L. Pyett, antique dealer*), and by Rufus, the handsomest white-and-gold tom in Hampstead, receiving homage from the passers-by on a farmhouse chair, set out for him every morning in the sun.

The shop-window was an endless source of wonder. It had neither shelves nor counters, but a window-seat ran across from end to end, littered with medleys of silver and trinkets and china, lace and embroideries, ornaments and small curios of all descriptions. Some were in trays, some in vaguely assorted heaps. You never quite knew what was good and what was only 'pretty trash' on the long low seat, where fine things took their chance in the higgledy-piggledy. Behind this vanguard the large open room was crowded with period and cottage furniture, laden indiscriminately with shawls, prints, musical boxes, objects in ivory, cloisonné, shagreen, glasses, punch-ladles, jewels, beads, and china, china, china. Colour rioted, lustres twinkled, and watchballs gave you a clue, if you knew how to take it. Almost always along the foreshore of the window-seat a kitten patted its way.

from "The Book of Hampstead," 1960

82

20, Perrin's Walk

CLOUGH WILLIAMS-ELLIS (1883-1978)

Architect, creator of Portmeirion, an Italianate town on the north-west coast of Wales, lived at Romney's House, Holly Bush Hill from 1929 until WW2.

The fine old house much altered and adapted to our curious habits,....
was....splendid....for large parties and we gave quite a lot of them—
dances every so often, a show by the Ballet Rambert, David Low drawing
large cartoons to amuse the company and selling them for charity.
We also gave a party to meet the Russian ambassador, M. Maisky, who
made a speech from the gallery balcony, and all sorts of odds and ends
of meetings and conferences, mostly cultural....

Whilst our children were still around Sir Solly Zuckerman wished one
of his research baboons on us, as he wanted to study its reactions to
'bright, intelligent young society'. He was then writing his rather
ambiguously entitled book 'The Sexual Life of Primates'— so his Betsy
had quarters on the flat roof at the top of the house for several months.
Not the social success we had hoped, unresponsive and dirty, we bade our
disappointing little lodger farewell without regrets. The experience
may have been good for Betsy but I don't think our children benefited
markedly from the association.

from "Architect Errant," 1971

84

ANNA WICKHAM (1884-1947)

Friend of <u>D.H. Lawrence</u> and Dylan Thomas. Studied singing, then married an astronomer by whom she had four sons. An ardent feminist who wished to fulfil herself as wife and mother as well as artist. Lived at 49, Downshire Hill and in Parliament Hill.

A HOUSE IN HAMPSTEAD

My house is damp as damp can be,
    It stands on London clay.
And if I move unthinkingly
    It shakes in a most alarming way,
Mayhap it will all come down on me
    One day.

But through the window I can see
    The most enchanting apple-tree.
In spring time, there are daffodils,
    And primroses on little hills,
And high within my apple-tree,
    A blackbird comes and sings to me:

On the black branch he sits and sings
    Of birds and nests and eggs and things.
I can't remember as I hear –
    That old grey London lies so near.

from "<u>The Man with a Hammer</u>"

GEORGE ORWELL (1903-1950)

Author of "Animal Farm," "1984" and other novels, essayist, columnist, occasional tramp. The bookshop where he once worked in South End Green is now a pizza bar.

MR. McKECHNIE'S BOOKSHOP

....The front room, unlike the rest of the shop was smart and expensive-looking, and it contained about two thousand books, exclusive of those in the window. On the right there was a glass showcase in which children's books were kept. Gordon averted his eyes from a beastly Rackhamesque dust-jacket; elvish children tripping Wendily through a bluebell glade. He gazed out through the glass door. A foul day, and the wind rising. The sky was leaden, the cobbles off the street were slimy. It was St. Andrew's day, the thirtieth of November. McKechnie's stood on a corner, on a sort of shapeless square where four streets converged. To the left, just within sight of the door, stood a great elm-tree, leafless now, its multitudinous twigs making sepia-coloured lace against the sky. Opposite, next to the Prince of Wales, were tall hoardings covered with ads for patent foods and patent medicines. A gallery of monstrous doll-faces – pink vacuous faces, full of goofy optimism....

from "Keep the Aspidistra Flying," 1936

88

JON KIMCHE (1909 –)

Journalist, ex-editor of "The Jewish Observer and Middle East Review."

MR. WESTROPE'S BOOKSHOP

.... Orwell and myself had a room there.... I used to work for the Westropes during the morning in payment for my rent, and Orwell used to work for them in the afternoon. He gives a very faithful description of the shop and the atmosphere in "Keep the Aspidistra Flying."

from a Letter to Ian Norrie, quoted in "The Book of Hampstead," 1960

PETER VANSITTART (1920–)

Author of more than twenty novels and of books for children. Teacher of English and history. Has lived in Hampstead since 1928.

TRADER BLAIR

In a dingy bookshop opposite the Playhouse Cinema, where I saw Judy Garland's first film, a tall, thin, abrupt man tried unsuccessfully to sell me "Trader Horn in Madagascar" when I wanted Wodehouse's "A Damsel in Distress." He was, one day, to send me the first book I ever reviewed, outside school, and, to my astonishment, paid me £1 : George Orwell.

Peter Vansittart, from "Paths From a White Horse," 1985

90

GEOFFREY GRIGSON (1905-1985)

Poet, anthologiser, prolific writer on many subjects, edited in the 1930s "New Verse" from his house in Keats Grove. Later moved to Wildwood Terrace, where he was a neighbour of Pevsner.

LOW COST OF LIVING

Hampstead in the Thirties was not an expensive place to live. It had its big houses for sure, its grand houses, but within easy distance of the tube station and the bus terminal plenty of Regency corners and little villa houses falling into shabbiness or decay and costing little to rent (or buy if you had the money). This high district was full of artists and writers of an older generation. Paul Nash lived (but rather well) in a biggish Edwardian house on Haverstock Hill. Orage, sunk now, I suppose, to an inhabitant only of other men's biographies and memoirs, fixed friends with his sharp eyes as they passed his garden gate at the bottom of Keats Grove. Higher up in John Street Edwin Muir was visible through cracked and unpainted French window frames, midnight after midnight, thumping out badly paid translations on a typewriter which seemed nearly as broken as the house.

from "Recollections," 1984

> John Street was an earlier name for Keats Grove, but Muir lived in Downshire Hill. A. R. Orage was editor of "The New Age".

EDWIN MUIR (1887-1959)

Poet, novelist, biographer, literary critic, lived at 7, Downshire Hill, in the 1930s, and described it in his "Autobiography," 1954.

The house itself was a source of happiness. It was an old dilapidated Strawberry Hill Gothic house, which vibrated gently whenever the underground train passed beneath it. A plumber and repairer had attended to it for an absent minded trust for forty years. Plumbing had developed during that time but he had not.... The lavatory pan swayed precariously when you sat on it. The garden at the back was filled with small bones and oyster-shells. An elderly lady who had the house before us had spent her days in bed, living on mutton-chops and oysters, and throwing the bones and shells through the open window....

Hampstead was filled with writing people and haunted by young poets despairing over the poor and the world, but despairing together, in a sad but comforting communion.

92

J. C. TREWIN (1908 -)

The Heath, they say, is Hampstead,
    The high-flung, spreading Heath,
With country airs about it
    And London's voice beneath;
Slim birch and tawny thicket,
    The Chilterns far beyond,
And sparrows in their congress
    Beside the Whitestone Pond.

The Heath, they say, is Hampstead,
    Yet I would rather go
(Begging their Lordships' pardon)
    At evening to Church Row
Where Time, in wig and ruffles,
    Sedately takes the air
With a Nubian page to bear the scythe
    Behind his gilded chair.
There Georgian brick remembers
    A cloudy swinging cane,
And Eliza Bennet whispers still
    To the listening ear of Jane.

Published in "The Observer" in the 1930s

The Lynds

ROBERT LYND (1879-1949)

Literary editor and essayist, married to <u>Sylvia Lynd</u>. When he first came to Hampstead he had rooms at 9, Gayton Road (see also <u>Melvyn Bragg</u>).

STOP PRESS

As an editor Black had only one fault. He was so restlessly energetic that he liked all copy to be in, not only punctually, but a considerable time before it was needed. I have often trembled as I lay in bed in my Hampstead lodgings on the morning of going-to-press day and heard him rushing up the stairs to put the inevitable question: 'Got your article finished?'

'It's under way', I would quaver from beneath the blankets. 'You mean you've got the title written', he would say disgustedly. Then, suddenly, the reign-of-terror frown would vanish, and he would leave the room laughing at his own perspicacity and at the hopelessness and helplessness of his friends.

from "<u>Life's Little Oddities</u>," 1941

[Ladbroke Black was assistant editor of "Today"; in his defence it should be noted that it was press day.]

DEDICATION

My dear Paul,

May I dedicate "_The Sporting Life_" to you, not because you catch an occasional fish in the intervals of painting, but because of the amusing days when we lived together in the same studio and owed money to the same milkman.

Yours,
Robert Lynd.

HAMPSTEADOPHOBIA

Hampsteadophobia is a disease common among taxi-drivers. The symptoms are practically unmistakable, though to a careless eye somewhat resembling those of apoplexy. At mention of the word "Hampstead" the driver affected gives a start, and stares at you with a look of the utmost horror. Slowly the blood begins to mount to his head, swelling first his neck and then distorting his features to twice their natural size. His veins stand out on his temples like bunches of purple grapes. His eyes bulge and blaze in their sockets....

I have often been puzzled as to the explanation of this. Is there some legend among taxi-drivers about a loathsome monster that lurks in the deeps of the Leg of Mutton Pond, and the mere sight of which causes madness in men of this particular calling? Or is their terror the result of some old story of a taxi-driver who once took a fare to Hampstead late at night and was never heard of again?

_from "_The Sporting Life_," 1922_

SYLVIA LYND (1887-1952)

Poet, novelist and short story writer, wife of Robert Lynd, was born at 11, Downshire Hill. After her marriage she lived at No. 14 and then at 5, Keats Grove.

14, Downshire Hill

SYLVIA LYND (1887~1952)

FIRST CONVERSION

When I was eleven two important events occurred; my Uncle Ger
had a bathroom built at 11, Downshire Hill; till then every night we
bathed, or a few years earlier were bathed, before the gas fire in my
mother's bedroom. After that we used the bathroom, with the excep-
tion of my father for whom a two-gallon can of hot water was carried
up every morning into his bedroom and who continued to use a sponge
bath drawn out from under his bed until the end of his life.

from "Slices of Autobiography," (unpublished)

FIRST RECOLLECTIONS

Almost my first memory must have been of the sensationally cold
winter of 1893 when a water-jug in those days of jugs and basins, broke
in two when it was lifted, and left a solid block of ice standing in the
basin. We had to draw water from a stand pipe in the road that winter,
and there were always people to put on one's skates beside the ponds on the
Heath. I remember still the horrible feeling of the screws going into the
heels of one's boots, and the black and white picture of the snowy world.
That winter killed the jasmine and the winter jasmine but it did not
kill the great wistaria at 11 Downshire Hill which is still growing and
flowering just as it used to.

from "Slices of Autobiography," (unpublished)

BASE DESIGN

After my English grandmother's death [c. 1876].... my Uncle George and my Uncle Frederick (always called by my sister and me Uncle Ger and Uncle Fer) and Aunt Bessie shared No. 5, Keats Grove.... [when the widow Wicher] married my Uncle Ger.... she wanted a house with big rooms in it like the one she had in Chalfont Gardens and as George Dryhurst had promised his sister Bessie that he would never leave her, in order that he might keep his word, he pulled down two little Regency houses next to 5, Keats Grove, called Britannia Villas, and built No. 6, Keats Grove on the site, employing for the purpose an architect who must have been the stupidest and silliest who ever lived. He built probably the last house with a basement built in London.

from "*Slices of Autobiography*," (unpublished)

Mrs. Dryhurst and her daughters; Nora (left) & Sylvia

WISTARIA

Like distant hills, like distant bells,
The misty-blue wistaria trails:
How tenderly they used to spread
Their leaves' light umber round my head.

There, as a child, I once would sit,
Holding a book, not reading it,
Within a lofty balcony,
Hung with the flowers' chalcedony.

Below me was a garden green,
Where many birds flew out and in;
And far outspread beyond the trees
Were London's roofs and belfries.....

Near me, my mother, whom I loved
About her bedroom lightly moved,
Or stood before the mirror there
Brushing and plaiting her long hair.

And if she sang or if she said,
Or if she sewed or if she read,
Her pleasure was made mine, and then
My pleasure increased hers again.

Old fans, old songs, old gaieties,
Old fables and embroideries,
With sunny mornings, in my mind,
And mist-blue flowers are intertwined.

And what delight would she make ours,
The first unfolding of the flowers.
Still I can see her as she stood
Rejoicing in each cadenced bud.

Still as she stood I see her stand
And stretch her white, life-giving hand
To touch the leafy tracery
That garlanded the balcony.

Beauty was first before my eyes
Made manifest in such a guise,
But what it was I did not guess,
For then its name was happiness.

In Memoriam, N.F.D.

N.F.D. was Sylvia Lynd's mother, a Dubliner who
married Dryhurst, secretary of the British Museum.
The wistaria still flourishes at 11, Downshire Hill.

NEIGHBOURS AT DOWNSHIRE HILL

But at the time of that 1898 bathroom other things were happening.
Chief of them was the Purcell Operatic Society, of which my mother,
N. F. Dryhurst, who loved everything to do with the theatre, and especially Ellen Terry, was made the Honorary Secretary, and Ellen Terry's
son, Gordon Craig, came to live at 8, Downshire Hill with Martin Shaw....
their charming Regency house....was white-washed throughout, and
given a dado of very dark brown paper.... The Purcell Operatic Society
seemed to justify whatever this supremely precious pair did by providing
them with a real secretary besides my delightful mother.... a gentle,
not to say insignificant little man whose name, Dolman, Gordon Craig
quickly transformed into Dormouse, and he loved to quote his frequent
response to any enquiry, 'You will find it, Mr. Craig, in the alcahove' –
an opening off the stairs used for stray junk....

He used to work in his upstairs room under a downpour of gas light....
There, as the summit of earthly happiness it seemed to me, would I be
sent for by Gordon Craig, whom I so much loved, as did all the feminine
creatures he met within those days (as in later and earlier ones) – I
would be sent for to paint his woodcuts to go out as advertisements of
the 'Book of Penny Toys'.

from "Slices of Autobiography," (unpublished)

104

GUESTS AT KEATS GROVE

How did the party end?

First with the arrival of <u>Victor</u>. Then with a grand confusion as to who should take the Beerbohms home. Finally Lionel did and the Davieses drove off with Sheila and left the Herberts behind, whom they should have taken too. This was bad staff work on my part. Then Robert insisted on bringing everyone who remained in again and a fierce argument about communism began between Alan and Victor with me putting in my oar in the cause of peace and occasional hope of bed. Alan was a little bit tight and rather rude. Peace being more or less preserved by 2 a.m., Rose rose to go. Then her car wouldn't start. Then everyone went to push it – then I quietly talking to <u>Victor</u>, who ceases to bluster and becomes nice when he is alone (Alan kept calling him and communists generally 'Smug' in a very annoying way) – Alan fell into the area but luckily did not hurt himself badly. Then we all went to push. Then the car was run down the hill – then – at last it was off – Rose and Bryan Guinness – Ruth and <u>Victor</u> – the Herberts in a taxi all the way to Hammersmith thanks to my meddling alas.

from <u>Diary</u> for October 21, 1935

> 'Rose' was Rose Macaulay, novelist; 'Alan', A.P.Herbert, lyricist, versifier; the 'Beerbohms' were incomparable.

MAIRE GASTER (1912 -)

Daughter of Robert and Sylvia Lynd, has lived most of her life in Hampstead. Formerly, a senior editor with William Heinemann.

JOYCE'S PARTY MUSIC

The high point of my mother's literary parties was undoubtedly the big party in 1931.... James Joyce was in London that summer, getting married to Nora Barnacle (after 36 years together) at Hampstead Town Hall (4th July, 1931) and they had their wedding lunch with the Lynds at 5 Keats Grove, along with their strangely silent grown-up children. The great party was a few days later. Douglas Jay and Goronwy Rees helped Sheila and me to prepare the fairy-lights, putting nightlights into little coloured thick glass jars with which to edge the flower-beds, and fixing Chinese lanterns in the weeping ash.

Sometime after midnight....we all went into the drawing-room....and then James Joyce went to the piano....

He sang 'Phil the Fluther's Ball' and I particularly remember the sad and beautiful 'Shule Aroon' –

> ' I'll dye my petticoats,
> I'll dye them red,
> And o'er the sea I'll beg my bread,
> And all my friends shall think me dead....'

Then Dominic Spring-Rice did some sort of recitation, looking, as J.B. Priestley said, 'like a maddened prawn', Johnny Morton (Beachcomber) sang his 'Blackwall Tunnel, that's the place for me....' and the evening ended with our playing the record of Anna Livia Plurabelle, himself reading it, which Joyce had just given my father.

from the Introduction to Sylvia Lynd's Autobiography (unpublished)

106

VICTOR GOLLANCZ (1893-1967)

Publisher, campaigner for human rights, nuclear disarmament, etc. Founder of The Left Book Club.

GOYS AND GOLLS

....we looked forward eagerly to her (Sylvia Lynd's) Friday nights: these were almost weekly when the season was right. There was a hard core, a crowd of casuals, and an occasional star: we were of the hard core, with Rose (his wife), the Priestleys, the Alan Thomases, the Norman Collinses, Humbert Wolfe and others. There was no one you might not meet there. Mark Gertler....the vastly entertaining Dulanty (who became Eire ambassador) and Johnny Morton – but he was a regular. So, almost was Sylvia's father, old Dryhurst.... He was a dull dry antisemite: I used to call him 'the old goy'. When the Lynd's second daughter became engaged to Jack Gaster he was outraged: "Once you had decided," he said, "to marry out of your race I could have wished you had chosen someone financially better based". On which Isaiah Berlin commented "Something in it, yes, yes. It's the job of a Jew to be rich".

.... The two stars I remember were Max Beerbohm and James Joyce. Humbert and I were lucky enough to please Max Beerbohm with a little dialogue in our best Jewish accents that ran like this:

> What sort of composer was Mozart?
> Mozart? *Mozart?* Rotten! Why, he wrote Faust.
> No, he didn't.
> What, he didn't even write Faust? Didn't I say he was a rotten composer?

(and, of Joyce)

Against his own low accompaniment he recited, though that is not the word, *Anna Livia Plurabelle*. He neither spoke it nor sang it: he used something like the sprechstimme, or pitch-controlled speech, familiar from *Moses and Aaron*, and other works by Schoenberg. And the sound of it was lovely beyond description.

from "*Reminiscences of Affection*", 1968

J. B. PRIESTLEY (1894-1984)

Novelist, dramatist, author of "The Good Companions," etc., lived at 27, Well Walk for a while in the early 1930s. His output was enormous but he had little to say about Hampstead. Maire Gaster was his editor at Heinemann.

LET THE AUTHOR SING

When I meet James Joyce in the solemn chapters of his American idolators, he seems monstrous, so narrow, humourless, arrogant. But that is what an idol should be. Probably, tongue in cheek, he offered them what they had gone all the way to Paris to find. In the reminiscences of his friends, Mary and Padraic Colum, we discover a very different character. So did I, the only time I spent an evening in his company. He was all amiability, and sang, in a pleasant light tenor, many comic songs. Probably it is too difficult to sing comic songs to pilgrims from American Eng. Lit. departments.

from "Margin Released," 1962

ARTHUR RANSOME (1884-1967)

Author of "Swallows and Amazons" and other immensely popular stories for children. Lived in Russia from 1913-1919 – hence "Old Peter's Russian Tales." Did not live in Hampstead but visited.

AT HOME TO POETS

Chelsea was always, so to speak, my home village, but I had friends also in Hampstead, which in those days was to Chelsea something of what Montmartre was to the Latin Quarter. The Dryhursts lived in Downshire Hill. Mrs. Dryhurst and her two daughters, Norah and Sylvia, were passionately Irish. Robert Lynd lived close by and he and Sylvia were friends of mine for nearly fifty years, indeed until they died. Mrs. Dryhurst had a 'day' (I forget which it was) and on that day her drawing-room was full of young people who, if not Irish, at least had no objection to Home Rule. There were always more of us than there were chairs, and poets used to read their poems aloud while we sat on the floor. At about six o'clock Mr. Dryhurst, who had never quite been forgiven for being English, used to come home from the British Museum, open the drawing-room door an inch or two, enough to look in on the Irishry, and disappear again at once.

from "Autobiography," 1976

Heathmen and Historians

JOHN STOW (c. 1525-1605)

London's first major historian whose "_Survey_" was published in 1598. He was a scholar who edited Chaucer and published a "_Chronicles_" and, later, an "_Annals of England_."

NOT SO FLEET

In the year 1589.... money amounting to a thousand marks, was collected, and it was undertaken, that by drawing divers springs about Hampstead heath into one head and course, both the city should be served of fresh water in all places of want; and also that by such a follower, as men call it, the channel of this brook should be scowered into this river of Thames; but much money being therein spent, the effect failed, so that the brook, by means of continual encroachment upon the banks getting over the water, and casting of soilage into the stream, is now become worse cloyed and choken than ever it was before.

from "_Stow's Survey of London_," 1598

114

CAROLINE A. WHITE (1810-1912)

Editor of "The Lady's Companion" for many years. Barratt quotes a poem she wrote on the eve of her hundredth birthday.

SECOND HOMES

After the Great Plague, change of air in the summer season became an article of faith with the inhabitants of London, and an annual sojourn of some weeks in the country or at the seaside an established custom with all who could afford it, a custom which resulted on the part of the wealthy merchants and citizens in the hire or purchase of a country retreat in one or other of the suburbs.

Hampstead, towards the end of the Commonwealth, combined the advantages of 'Air and Hill, and Well and School', and these favourable circumstances, added to its easy distance from London, recommended it to the City fathers and mothers, and made it, of all the rural villages in the neighbourhood of town, the most popular.

from "Sweet Hampstead and its Associations," 1900

JOHN JAMES PARK (1795-1833)

Wrote the first history of Hampstead when he was only 19, his delicate health having confined him to his father's house at 18, Church Row. He was called to the bar and, during his brief life, wrote extensively about the law.

GENTLEMEN FARMERS

The village of Hampstead has been peculiarly attractive to commercial and professional men; and the operation of wealth is strongly perceivable in the condition of its landed property. To those who have acquired opulence in this way, the possession of a country villa is incomplete without the addition of something which may be called *a farm*. The adjoining land-owner probably knows his own interest too well to reject the advantageous proposal; and hence a portion of his estate is subtracted, and conveyed over to his exulting neighbour.

PRE-CENTRALLY-HEATED HAMPSTEAD

The atmosphere of Hampstead is, as may be expected from it's (sic) situation, dry and keen, and is said by Dr. Soame to resemble that of Montpelier. Yet, though it may appear paradoxical, I have not the least hesitation in asserting that Hampstead is frequently warmer than London in the winter season. I have even heard it said by a person who kept one thermometer at Hampstead and another in London, and travelled between the two places daily, that he almost uniformly found his own town thermometer lower than his country one. We may, perhaps, account for the penetrating *out-door* cold of London, by considering that the atmosphere there is filled with particles of moisture, so small as to be imperceptible to the eye, which, becoming frozen in severe weather, add extremely to the sharpness of the air. Within doors, I believe London to be invariably warmer than Hampstead.

from "The Topography and Natural History of Hampstead," 1814

Dr. John Soame was champion of the Hampstead waters during the second period of the Wells.

117

F. E. BAINES (1832 – 1911)

Pioneer of the post-office telegraph system who also became inspector general of mails and wrote a two-volume work on <u>Forty Years at the Post-Office</u>. He was living in Park Road (now Parkhill Road) off Haverstock Hill, in 1889.

LATE VICTORIAN STATISTICS

For electoral purposes Hampstead is divided into four wards. The Town Ward comprises the highest ground of the parish, together with the ancient village of Hampstead and the houses bordering the Heath. It contains 2556 houses rated to the relief of the poor. The Belsize Ward covers the lower slopes on the southern side with 1679 houses. The Adelaide Ward includes all the rest of the borough east of the Finchley Road. It contains 1180 houses. Finally the Kilburn Ward covers all the parish west of the Finchley Road and Finchley New Road: it contains no fewer than 3721 houses.

Altogether the parish covers an area of 2248 acres with 9136 houses. The exact population is as yet indeterminate. It has largely increased since the census of 1881, and may be reasonably estimated at about 67,000 persons at Lady-day of 1889.

from "<u>Records of Hampstead</u>," 1890

118

PARK OR HEATH?

Hampstead itself, now a town of 80,000 people, is almost entirely modern; the old village has been gradually destroyed until there is next to nothing left. But the Heath remains, the only wild piece of land within easy reach of the Londoner. It remains to be seen whether the authorities will continue to observe the difference between a park and a heath.

G. E. Mitton, from "Hampstead: The Fascination of London" (ed. Besant), 1902

EIGHTY YEARS ON

PARLIAMENT HILL FIELDS
Welcome to Your Park

This notice, with variations ushering you on to the West Heath, the East Heath, and elsewhere, is displayed at many entrances to London's largest tract of open land because the administrators of the Greater London Council have not learned to distinguish between a park and a heath.

Ian Norrie, from "Hampstead: London Hill Town," 1982

SIR WALTER BESANT (1836-1901)

Wrote fiction, mainly historical, literary criticism and works about the Holy Land. He was President of the Palestine Exploration Fund, 1868-86. A street in West Hampstead is named after him. 18, Frognal End was built for him in 1892. A founder of the Society of Authors, 1884.

HOME OR HAME, HAM'S BEST

The name of this borough is clearly derived from "ham", or "hame", a home; and "steede", a place, and has consequently the same meaning as homestead. Park, in a note in his book on Hampstead, says that the "p" is a modern interpolation, scarcely found before the seventeenth century, and not in general use until the eighteenth.

G.E. Mitton, from "Hampstead: The Fascination of London" (ed. Besant), 1902

18, Frognal End

THOMAS J. BARRATT (1841-1914)

An advertising impresario who worked for Pears, started the famous "Cyclopaedia" and sold soap with the aid of Millais' "Bubbles." Spent part of his private fortune on amassing Hampsteadiana, later bequeathed to the Council as the Bellmoor Collection. There is a plaque to him on the neo-Tudor flats at the top of East Heath Road, where he lived from 1877 until his death. His three-volume history was reprinted in facsimile in 1972.

BARRATT'S EARLY DAYS

For the best part of my life I have been a resident in Hampstead, on the high vantage ground of the Heath. Familiar with the place from boyhood, it is endeared to me by many personal memories. I seem to have known it always. About its fair and spacious Heath, and over all parts of its lovely surroundings, I used to ramble and play in my youth. There was hardly a tree I did not know; many of them it was my delight, with other boys, to climb, to see whose name should be carved nearest to the topmost bough. I remember the Gospel Oak fields — unsurpassable, it seemed to me, in vernal beauty and floral radiance — before the railway was cut through them. There I gathered flower and plant specimens for my botanical lessons, and skimmed the ponds for objects for the microscope. And from that time to the present I have been more or less closely connected with this time-honoured and beautiful suburb.

from Preface to "The Annals of Hampstead," 1912

122

C.E.M. JOAD (1891-1953)

Popular philosopher and writer, one of the original members of the BBC Brains Trust. He lived at No. 4, East Heath Road, for many years, sharing the accommodation during WW2 with Kingsley Martin, editor of "The New Statesman".

BATHING AT HAMPSTEAD

I often go to the open-air bathing-pools on Hampstead Heath. On the Hampstead side there is only one in which bathing is permitted, but it is a very lovely pool, fringed with rushes and flowering shrubs, and in springtime gay with lilac, laburnum and May blossom. Men and women are not permitted to bathe there on the same day, four days being set apart for the men and two for the women. Apparently it is thought to be wicked at Hampstead for men and women to see the outlines of one another's bodies, even when veiled by regulation costumes....

But that what is wicked in Hampstead should be at the same time observed as a respectable, social function a few miles away at Hornsey is surprising, and throws an interesting light on the moral foibles of borough (or should it be county?) councillors. I asked the attendant at the Hampstead ponds why mixed bathing was not permitted, and quoted the Hornsey precedent. He said that mixed bathing might be all very well at Hornsey, but that it wouldn't do at Hampstead because of the riff-raff.

from "The Book of Joad," 1932

124 [*The regulations were relaxed some years later.*]

JOHN LE CARRE (1931 –)

Novelist, ex-teacher, member of HM Foreign Service, 1960-4. Author of "The Spy Who Came in From the Cold," "Tinker, Tailor, Soldier, Spy," etc. His latest, "A Perfect Spy" is due to be published in March 1986. Lived for many years at No. 1, Gayton Crescent before moving 'elsewhere in Hampstead' in the late 1970s.

A CORPSE BY THE BOUNDARY PATH

'Knew him personally at all, did you, sir?' The Detective Chief Superintendent of Police asked respectfully in a voice kept deliberately low. 'Or perhaps I shouldn't enquire.'

The two men had been together for fifteen minutes but this was the Superintendent's first question. For a while Smiley did not seem to hear it, but his silence was not offensive, he had the gift of quiet. Besides, there is a companionship about two men contemplating a corpse. It was an hour before dawn on Hampstead Heath, a dripping, misty, no-man's hour, neither warm nor cold, with a heaven tinted orange by the London glow, and the trees glistening like oilskins. They stood side by side in an avenue of beeches and the Superintendent was taller by a head: a young giant of a man, prematurely grizzled, a little pompous perhaps, but with a giant's gentleness that made him naturally befriending. Smiley was clasping his pudgy hands over his belly like a mayor at a cenotaph, and had eyes for nothing but the body lying at his feet in the beam of the Superintendent's torch. The walk this far had evidently winded him, for he puffed a little as he stared. From the darkness round them, police receivers crackled on the night air. There were no other lights at all; the Superintendent had ordered them extinguished.

'He was just somebody I worked with,' Smiley explained after a long delay.

from "Smiley's People," 1980

C.W. IKIN (1921 -)

Solicitor, long-term member of the Heath and Old Hampstead Society. Has dwelt, all his life, close to the Heath in Wildwood Road and Wildwood Rise. In 1971, for the centenary of the Act which preserved the Heath, he wrote a book about how it was saved for the public. It was reprinted, with some revisions, in 1985.

LOST MOORLAND

.... My own personal regret is that the Sandy Heath, West Heath and Upper East Heath are no longer moorland, as they were from 1680 to 1890, for woodland can easily be found round London and moorland cannot. I regret too that country meadows, hedged, and with rough grass, are now so rare on the Heath. Many former meadows of this type are now either scrub woodland or open park. I would also dearly like to see a long-term plan to restore not only the Georgian landscaping of the Kenwood, Fitzroy and Evergreen Hill estates.... but also the Capability Brown design of Golders Hill.

from "Hampstead Heath", 1985

CHRISTOPHER WADE (1921–)

*Compiler of the Camden History Society's "Streets"
series, ex-publications officer of the Camden History
Society, curator of The Hampstead Museum, Burgh
House. Has lived in Willoughby Road since 1956.
Formerly with the B.B.C.*

NAME BUT NOT HOUSE DROPPING

Rather than pure name-dropping, which some decry but enjoy just
the same, I have tried to find out why the famous came to Hampstead
and what they did while here: also what effect they had on the
neighbourhood and vice versa. In the case of the artists and writers,
who pepper these pages, I have explored their relevant works and noted
some of their reflections on Hampstead. Constable's views of the
Heath are well known, but not so D.H.Lawrence's short story set in
Heath Street and Orwell's mockery of Willoughby Road. I have not
included the many famous people who currently live in Hampstead
for the sake of their peace and privacy.

from "The Streets of Hampstead," rev. ed. 1984

MICHAEL FOOT (1913 –)

M.P., privy councillor, journalist and biographer of Swift and Aneurin Bevan. Has lived in Hampstead for more than twenty years. A dedicated walker on the Heath.

Photograph by **NIGEL SUTTON,** *Ham & High*

HEATHMAN MEETS HEATHMAN

"Who is the sorrel nag?" I heard a familiar voice, half knowing, half curious, cry out across the Heath. Perhaps there was a touch of mockery too, and that should have put me on my guard.

It was the voice of John Hillaby, who knows every twist and turn of Hampstead Heath and, best of all, as the greatest of all Heath-lovers, Leigh Hunt, put it: "And that clear path through all, where daily meet/Cool cheeks, and brilliant eyes, and morn-elastic feet." He is also, let me remind you – Hillaby, not Hunt – the most formidable collector of miscellaneous, useless knowledge. Each adjective is intended as a compliment.

He was now parading his comprehension of Gulliver's Travels, a theme on which I counted myself the expert, at least in our part of the Heath near South End Green, if not across the whole 800-odd acres of holy ground.

CLIO CON BRIO

However, let us ensure above all else in this millennial year that proper tribute is paid to the historians. Poets, painters, publicans, publicists, even politicians have all contributed to the glory of Hampstead, and each will receive a passing salute, but the historians of Hampstead are a breed all their own, from James Park to Ian Norrie.

Every favourite corner or grotto on Hampstead Heath offers a dozen different entrances and exits; and the Hampstead historians offer a similar criss-cross of pathways, leading inconsequentially to a multitude of new names and discoveries.

from "A Hymn for Hampstead – or 986 and all that", Ham and High,
10.1.86

131

HUNTER DAVIES (1936-)

Journalist, broadcaster, novelist and author of books about the Beatles, the Lakes, Hadrian's Wall, the London Parks, etc. Married to novelist Margaret Forster. Lived at 9, Heath Villas, Vale of Health, from 1960-1963, before moving to Kentish Town.

WALKERS ON THE HEATH

I have lived beside the Heath since 1960 and I estimate I have put in 10,000 walking hours, doing a morning and afternoon walk each day, plus three hours on Sunday playing football.... We regular Heath-walkers, we like to think we know everything and everyone, we nod and smile, without knowing names or background, recognising each other by an angle of the body, the dog on the lead, the time of the day, that path they always come down. We see it in all weathers, all seasons, and know what used to be beside that pond, behind those trees, what will happen in the coming season to those meadows, what will appear on that hill, where the dragonflies play, changes for the better, changes for the worse, we've seen them come, we've seen them go....

I know people who live on the Hampstead side who never walk on our side, always keeping on the heights, avoiding the hoi polloi down below near Highgate Road. John Le Carre and John Hillaby are both regular Heath-walkers, but I've never seen them on the Kentish Town side. Michael Foot, with his Welsh terrier Disraeli, does venture our way, on his marathon Heath walks, but he has other things to occupy him recently. A. J. P. Taylor lives on our side and is one of the masses. He goes everywhere, including regular dips in the open air pond.

132   *from "A Walk Round London's Parks," 1983*

John Hillaby

F. M. L. THOMPSON (1925 –)

Professor of Modern History at Bedford College, London, from 1968, commissioned by the last Council of Hampstead to write a history of the Borough. Also author of "English Landed Society in the Nineteenth Century."

THE BEST OF PRIZES

The broad lines of the portrait of Hampstead can be indicated very simply. Until the late seventeenth century it was simply high, rather than high-class or residential, and there is little to suggest that its history was substantially different from that of any other place within three to five miles of the City and Westminster. From then until the early nineteenth century the distinctive character of old Hampstead was formed, as a satellite town of the metropolis, separated from it by open and generally steeply-sloping fields. By the 1820s the metropolitan building tide reached the southern shores of the parish, and from then until the early 1900s washed over it. Before 1914 the tide had passed on, lapping in this north-westerly direction at Golders Green, Willesden, Hendon and Finchley, and leaving behind it Hampstead fully developed apart from its great prize, Hampstead Heath.

from "Hampstead: Building a Borough, 1650-1964," 1974

JOHN RICHARDSON (1935 -)

Former councillor of both St. Pancras and Camden, chairman of the Camden History Society which he founded in 1970. He is a publisher and author and wrote the most recent history of "Highgate".

STANDING ORDERS

The conservation debate rages frequently in Hampstead. The older, more picturesque houses of the town are now so well guarded, at least against demolition, that it is difficult to imagine any more of them disappearing, unless by some illegal action. Legislation has helped, but Hampstead has been particularly fortunate in its watchdog, the Heath and Old Hampstead Society....

The complaint of modern architects is that areas like Hampstead can become ossified, with change rejected for the sake of it. They can point, with justification, to some very good modern buildings in the borough....

It is a dilemma for planner and architect, for whom it used to be customary in the 1960s to think in terms of replenishment of housing stock within sixty years or so. As Hampstead reaches its one thousandth recorded year many of its properties have stood for at least a fifth of that span and are now protected in perpetuity. How long will it be before the formal but homely and pleasant terraces of Belsize and Chalcots are thought of in the same way? The question must be asked: is this what we want?

from "Hampstead One Thousand, AD 986-1986," 1985

135

IAN NORRIE (1927-)

Author/editor of several books on Hampstead, London, Europe, chronicler of the twentieth-century book trade, managing director of the High Hill Bookshop.

LOW PROFILE

Hampstead has not figured prominently in the history of Great Britain. No battle is known to have been fought here, and royal visits have been infrequent, although royal underwear came here regularly during the reign of Henry VIII, and subsequently, for the attention of native laundresses, who dried it upon the Heath. There has never been an Edict of Hampstead, nor a Council (except in the parochial or bureaucratic sense), nor a Conference, although it had its own mock parliament for more than half-a-century, seriously debating the great issues of the day in imitation of the House of Commons. There is no Duke, nor has there been, no Earl, no Count or Countess, but today when the creation of life peerages is said to be causing a shortage of desirable titles, there are two lords and one lady of Hampstead. I wonder how many could name them?

from "Hampstead: London Hill Town," 1982

A. ALVAREZ (1929-)

Poet, author, journalist, has lived in Hampstead since the early 1930s., when his nanny walked him on the Heath every day. Now he walks his dog there. Books include "The Savage God" and "Offshore." The following passage comes from an essay written for "Esquire" in 1984.

Having Hampstead Heath on your doorstep means you can go for a long country walk right in the middle of London. Sometimes, when the wind is in the west, you can hear the faint hum of traffic, but usually there is no way of guessing that beyond the fields and sheltering trees is a city of almost seven million people. On a wet February afternoon, when the leaves are gone, and the east wind freezes the rain on your fingers, and the gulls, blown in from the sea, are swooping and squabbling above the long stretch of sodden grass that slopes down to the Highgate ponds, the place seems as remote and desolate as Hardy's Egdon Heath.

It is also safe. I suppose it is typical of the sly British psyche that although the Heath is crawling with nuts – flashers displaying themselves to young mothers pushing prams, peeping toms who make every courting couple's life a misery – nobody actually gets mugged. Hampstead Heath may have changed since Keats and Coleridge walked on it together, but it has not otherwise, thank God, entered the twentieth century.

LETTICE COOPER (1897–)

Novelist, President of International Pen, 1977-9, contributor to the "Times Literary Supplement," "The Observer," etc. Author of "Fenny," "National Provincial," her first novel was published in 1925, her twentieth, "Unusual Behaviour" is scheduled for June, 1986. Resident in West Hampstead since 1945.

VIEW OF THE VALE

Where the Heath slopes down from the Spaniards to the Vale of Health, Alan sat on a hump of grass trying to make up his mind to go and see Vida that afternoon. Behind him the sparse fir trees stirred in a gentle breeze. Drifts of scent came to him from a rounded hawthorn bush heavy with flower. Far off over Ken Wood a cuckoo called. London lay stretched out below him in a haze the colour of harebells. In the valley the roundabouts were still, but in his mind was a roundabout that would not stop turning.

from "Black Bethlehem", 1947

[*Spaniards is novelist's-licence for Jack Straw's Castle.*]

138

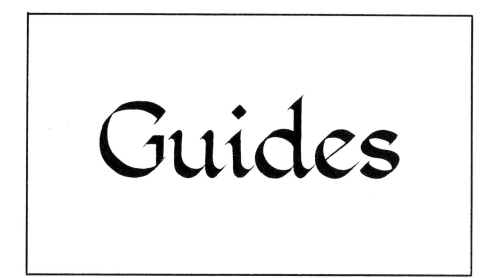

Guides

Nikolaus Pevsner   *Photograph by Frank Herrmann*

SIR NIKOLAUS PEVSNER (1902-1983)

Architectural historian and commentator, sometime Slade Professor of Fine Art at Cambridge and Professor of the History of Art at Birkbeck, London, author of "The Outline of European Architecture", "Pioneers of Modern Design", editor of "The Pelican History of Art and Architecture", and of "The Buildings of England", twenty-nine volumes of which he was the sole author. Lived in Hampstead, at 2, Wildwood Terrace, North End, from 1936 until his death.

CARTOGRAPHER'S NIGHTMARE

Perhaps the most remarkable thing about Hampstead Village is that it has kept its street pattern, very close and intricate, so much so that the designers of the average street atlas of London declare themselves defeated by it and substitute an odd pattern without names for the dozens of narrow passages, stepped lanes, and tiny squares.

WEST HAMPSTEAD, that is, the district W of Finchley Road, need be visited only by those in search of Victorian churches. The houses and streets require no notice.

> Despite expressing the latter opinion Sir Nikolaus accepted an invitation to launch the only book so far published on the subject – "The Streets of West Hampstead." At a party in the Ham & High offices, in 1975, having climbed a staircase to address the audience, he remarked, 'Now you see the ruin on the hill'.

from "The Buildings of England: London (except the Cities of London and Westminster)," 1952

140

PRE-JUGGERNAUT HAMPSTEAD

Of all the boroughs of N London Hampstead has most visibly preserved its C18 character of a favourite villeggiatura near town, for the summer months or for retirement. This is due to two causes: the 'green bar' of Regent's Park, Primrose Hill, and Hampstead Heath between London and Hampstead, and the steepness of the hill on which the village lies. A hill (see Harrow, Middlesex) if steep enough to rule out trams and buses is bound to help in keeping the character of a place from adulteration.

[Buses, even double-deckers, have since invaded the village.]

CONGREGATIONAL CHURCH, LYNDHURST ROAD

....by Waterhouse, one of his most satisfactory works. Purple brick and majolica decoration, lancet windows, round-arched; round-arched entrance. Clear, hard, and rigid....

TOWN HALL, HAVERSTOCK HILL

1875, by Kendall & Maw. Red brick and stone, Italianate. Crushingly mean; a disgrace to so prosperous and artistic a borough.

from "The Buildings of England: London" (except the Cities of London & Westminster), 1952

IAN NAIRN (1930-1983)

Journalist who specialised in architecture. Joint author, with Nikolaus Pevsner, of the Surrey and Sussex volumes in the "Buildings of England" series. He did not live in Hampstead.

HAMPSTEAD VILLAGE

Hampstead is a bit of a joke, though many of its inhabitants are deadly serious about it. As soon as a picturesque street or alley gets well started and you can begin to live the refined life, along comes a great hospital or board school or block of tenements. Clatter and thump, you pick up the pieces and start again. It is not an amusing or exciting contrast, either, just head-on conflict which ends in stalemate. But socially, it has undoubtedly saved Hampstead from becoming intolerably precious.

The maze of alleyways and passages is still all there, behind the heavy through traffic in Heath Street, but only once does it add up to something. This is in Holly Mount, and the way to get to it is up a set of steps between 73 and 75 Heath Street, near the Cruel Sea. The staircase winds round, giving you a tiptoe peep down Rosslyn Hill, and then deposits you in a tiny hilltop square, apparently a hundred miles from the lorries, with a good pub (the Holly Bush) which has been left alone by the bright boys. Here, the traditional idea of Hampstead really comes alive. But a few steps farther, towards Mount Vernon, and the colossal bulk of the National Institute for Medical Research shatters this highly-strung small-scale elegance. The whole place is a china shop with a good many wild bulls in it.

from "Nairn's London", 1966

144

SIMON JENKINS (1943-)

Commentator on the London scene as author and journalist. Editor of the "Evening Standard," 1976-8, now political editor of the "Economist," author of "Images of Hampstead," 1982. Resident of NW1 (Regent's Park) for many years.

BUILT TO LAST

Hampstead is an easy place with which to fall in love. It offers the perfect fusion of urban bustle and rural privacy, as if all the elements of English townscape had been tossed in the air and fallen on this hillside with hardly a piece out of place. The people of Hampstead – pump-room rowdies, 'Bohemian' commuters, left-wing intellectuals – are merely its passing phantoms. The lasting Hampstead is a maze of steps, alleyways, turnings and sudden views. It is sprays of clematis, wistaria, ivy and holly scattering sunlight on to red brick and white stucco. It is grand mansions, terraced cottages, Victorian extravagance and workhouse simplicity contained within a surprisingly intact eighteenth- and nineteenth-century hill town, defended on three sides by a rambling heath and on the fourth by the stern ramparts of Italianate Belsize Park. The twentieth century has lobbed an occasional grenade over these ramparts. But Hampstead's defenders have become increasingly adept at lobbing them back. For once, it is probable that the town we see today is the town we shall bequeath to our descendants.

from "Companion Guide to Outer London," 1981

146

SIR DAVID PIPER (1918-)

Director of the Ashmolean, 1973-85; Fellow of Worcester College, Oxford, since 1973. Author of "Enjoying Painting," "The English Face", etc.

THE CHELSEA CONNECTION

The village of Hampstead boomed early in the eighteenth century, and became almost a spa.... Now it is closest in atmosphere to Chelsea, but a hill-borne, airy Chelsea, full of pretty houses, painted up to the nines, narrow streets angled steeply up and down, and evidence of prosperous art and intellect (recently the admirable High Hill Bookshop bore a notice, 'Children of Progressive Parents admitted only on Leads') and full of money.

from "Companion Guide to London," 6th ed., 1977

SEZ WHO?

Though they're far apart the atmosphere is similar in these two districts of London. In fact Chelsea is often called the Hampstead along the Thames and Hampstead the Chelsea of the North.

from Berlitz Guide to "London," 1985/6

IVOR BROWN (1891-1974)

Dramatic critic, essayist, novelist, biographer of "Shakespeare", author of numerous books about words, editor of "The Observer" during the 1940s, a Scot who lived much of his life in Hampstead. Married to Irene Hentschel, the theatrical director, they lived for long at 20, Christchurch Hill.

'SOME MELODIOUS PLOT'

Keats House in Hampstead is the authentic habitation and work-shop of the genius whom Hampstead air could not save from his tuberculosis…. The House lies on the south-eastern edge of the Heath and the nightingale, which moved Keats to write his famous ode, has no descendants to sing there now. But it remains a semi-rural villa, well preserved, first with handsome American aid, by the Hampstead Borough Council. It shows the usual type of relic, letters, pictures, first editions and writing desk. It is not a dusty museum of letters, but a living centre of readership, since there is a branch of the bor-ough's public library next to the Keatsian portion.

from "Cities of Enchantment, LONDON," 1960

148

ALASTAIR SERVICE (1933-)

Author of many books and articles on architects and architecture, and also on pre-history. He is presently Director of the Family Planning Association. Has lived in Hampstead for much of his life, in Redington Road, Flask Walk, etc.

WELLS AND BATHS

Standing on the Flask Walk green, we can also look up hill and see signs of why Hampstead is the mixed-class community it is today. The Georgian houses belong to actors, writers, poets and the like, but above these we can see the threatened working class dwellings of New Court (the larger block 1854, the smaller 1871), both the idea of the solicitor Hugh Jackson, father of Sir T. G. Jackson, the noted architect who re-built much of Hampstead Parish Church, the splendid New End Schools (T. J. Bailey and the LCC schools architect, 1903, in a Baroque manner of truly Edwardian flamboyance) and, in Flask Walk itself, the muscular Wells and Campden Baths and Wash-house (as inscribed on charitable red brick), designed by Henry Legg, 1888. For ninety years, this building provided austerely hygienic baths for the people in the bath-less working class tenements up the hill – an odd successor to the fashionable Spa buildings along the road – before conversion into private houses in 1981.

from "A Walk Through Victorian and Edwardian Hampstead", to be published in 1987.

150

John & Wendy Trewin (Photo: Mark Trewin)

J.C. TREWIN (1908–)

Dramatic critic and author has lived with his wife, Wendy, at various Hampstead addresses since 1938. In an autobiography, "Down to the Lion", 1952, he wrote the accompanying extract.

I had met Hampstead first on an August day in the 1930s, just after coming to London, when the City was like some Eugene O'Neill stokehold. Escaping on a vague 'story' to get out of the way of a fussy acting news editor, I spent most of the day somewhere between Ken Wood and the Vale of Health, where the Heath swelled into gentle green crests.... Later I wandered among the silver-birch coppices and the rumpled glades, and through the tangle of step-and-lane in the old village; I found the elegance of Church Row with the Parish Church at the foot, and Tree's grave over the way, and went across to the Regency grace of Downshire Hill and Keats Grove. I knew that one day I must live in Hampstead....

Some years later we did....

We have known Hampstead from a modern cellular flat; a house where Clarkson Stanfield, the scene-painter, Macready's friend, once lived; a cheer-fully sprawling upper-part looking towards the tower of the Parish Church on the rise; and a tranquil house not very far from the garden where Keats heard the nightingale....

152

WENDY TREWIN (1915 –)

Author of "All on Stage: Charles Wyndham and the Alberys," etc. and editor of "The Journals of Caroline Fox." "Embroidered Church Kneelers" (with Barbara Thomson) will be published soon.

August 24: Bought curtains this morning to darken our windows. Half of Hampstead has done the same. The man in the shop said to the woman in front of me: 'not meaning to be rude, Madam, I must point out that you have had three months in which to buy material for this purpose....*

August 25: Hotter and hotter. Tenser and tenser. Had a disturbed night. J. saw a man crouching outside our kitchen window. We called the police who came very rapidly, shone torches all over the black-out, and found nothing.

August 26: The Heath, except for a crowd round the balloon barrage operations, almost empty. Whitestone Pond, usually with a dozen yachts on a fine Saturday evening, had one. So many children already gone away, I suppose.

from 1939 Diary quoted in J. C. Trewin's "Down to the Lion," 1952

PETER VANSITTART (1920 –)

RETURN TO NORMAL

Throughout war-time changes of address, I had maintained a Hampstead base. Returning permanently in 1947, I found few very startling changes. Sunday morning bugles still rang for some unseen parade. Each day I was awoken by unseen horses trotting up Heath Street to the Whitestone Pond, where, later, raucous Mosleyites would gather, as they had done in the thirties. Tennis courts, the Everyman, British Restaurants, Salvation Army, people in dressing gowns buying early bread in the High Street, small tea shops managed by genteel ladies, old-fashioned drapers, still remained, apparently unthreatened. On a Heath bench, as if he had been sitting there throughout the war, was the dirty-bearded, red-eyed, many-coated and well-papered tramp I had long known.... The Heath was as ever: the kites still floated above Parliament Hill, the blue and yellow balls rose and fell behind a dark copse. A woman paused to tell me that, when a child, she had imagined that 'going on holiday' meant living in a distant ash visible across the Heath from her bedroom.

from "_Paths From a White Horse_," 1985

KENNETH CLARK, (LORD CLARK) (1903-1979)

Art historian, sometime Director of the National Gallery, author and presenter of the BBC-TV series "Civilisation." Lived briefly at Capo di Monte, Windmill Hill in the 1940s, until he moved to Upper Terrace House, where he remained for many years.

GRACIOUS LIVING

Opposite our small, romantic Capo di Monte was a large walled garden in which stood a modernised eighteenth-century house, called Upper Terrace House. As the inconvenience of our pretty deceiver became more apparent to us we began to cast lustful eyes on this almost too obviously 'desirable' residence. The owner had fled to Barbados, and ultimately we were able to buy it for a sum that then seemed large, but would now be considered ridiculously small. The house had been 'made over' by an architect without convictions named Oliver Hill, who practised in a 'modern style' so contrived as to put conventional people at ease. The staircase was hideous, but looked very solid, and we sat under it during the occasional air raid warning. The garden was charming, and became Jane's chief delight. We thought that we should live there for ever. Our first act was to bring our pictures from Upton. Renoir's 'Baigneuse Blonde' hung over the chimney piece in the sitting room, and was the tutulary goddess of the house. We brought her up in 1943 to greet our new friend, René Massigli, the first French Ambassador to England under the de Gaulle régime.

from "The Other Half," 1977

156

Upper Terrace House

ERNEST RAYMOND (1888-1974)

Author of "<u>We, the Accused</u>," "<u>Tell England</u>," "<u>Mr. Olim</u>," "<u>A Georgian Love Story</u>" and many other novels. Came to live in Hampstead in August 1940 at 9, Gardnor Mansions, Church Row. Moved, in 1941, to 22, The Pryors, East Heath Road, where he died. Liberal Member of the last Hampstead Borough Council, 1962-1965.

His novel, "<u>The Corporal of the Guard</u>," is set in Hampstead (therein disguised as Hodden Moor) and is based on his Home Guard experiences in the second world war. The accompanying extract comes from "<u>An Old Platoon</u>," an essay contributed to "<u>The Book of Hampstead</u>" (1960).

158

They were drawn from every class, party, religion, profession and trade – even from more than one nationality. I remember amongst them several lawyers, civil servants, bank clerks, big-business men and small shop-keepers; a publisher, an editor, a labourer, a brewer, and a verger. At first they went to their assemblies with only a white brassard and the letters L.D.V. (Local Defence Volunteers) on one arm; later, in full service uniform, they came to be called No. 15 Company, 20th Middlesex Regiment, Home Guard; and their task was nothing less than to defend Hampstead and its splendid open spaces from any airborne enemy that 'dared invade the borders of their realm'.

Since I was but a rank-and-file unit in No. 1 Platoon of that company, later known as A Platoon, it is only of this particular brotherhood that I can speak with any assurance that I am talking truth and sense (so obscure are his military performances to a mere ranker).

When a German invasion of England still seemed a likely affair, say in 1940 and '41, it was plain that the great open spaces which are the glory of Hampstead and its neighbourhood – the Heath, Kenwood Fields, Kenwood Park, Parliament Fields, Parliament Hill – were possible landing grounds for parachute of airborne troops during an attempted attack on London in its broad vale, down below these Northern Heights. With any such insolent operation our No. 15 Company was trained and equipped – and eager – to interfere. Every one of those open spaces was for us a field of fire. On a dozen rises and ridges in Parliament Fields, Kenwood Fields and Kenwood Park slit trenches were sited for us by the Brigade of Guards (who should know their job, but of course we old sweats bitterly criticized their siting) and from these grave-like trenches we were prepared to sweep all the areas before us with such a cross-fire that few, if any, of our visitors should escape these killing-grounds. If any did escape, say into the cover of Ken Wood itself, why then we had our mobile reserve and counter-attack parties to beat the wood, find them, and deal with them there.

DIANA RAYMOND (1916~)

Author of more than twenty novels including "The Small Rain", "Emma Pride", and "Strangers' Gallery", which is partly set in 'Hampstead', the Salutation Hill noted in the accompanying extract having close resemblances to Downshire Hill. She has lived in Hampstead since 1940 when she married Ernest Raymond.

ONLY FOUR MILES FROM THE CENTRE

At noon in summer Salutation Hill ran with a scented expectant silence, like a road that leads down to the sea. The light walls of the Regency houses, the paved front gardens, and the trees in tubs and the jewelled window-boxes, the occasional licked-lollipop scarlet of a front door below a fanlight delicate as the skeleton of a bird, all wore a clear sea-fresh light, while in the pad of sandals on dry pavements was the sound of children running to the shore. Amongst the tricycles and woollen rabbits abandoned in the paved yards lay sometimes a bucket and spade, though the only sand to be gathered here was the thin soil between the paving-stones, or the summer dust in the road.

Residents turning to their guests at the chosen spot where the end of the road was filled with a sight of the old Salutation Inn (where Dr. Johnson had come, and where Keats had heard, if not the nightingale, a nightingale), the blond dried grasses of the Heath and a surprising depth of sky, would say, 'You'd never believe you were only four miles from the centre of London, would you?'

There was no Inn at the end of Downshire Hill in the 18th C. Samuel Johnson drank at the Upper Flask at the top of Heath Street and Keats is popularly supposed to have heard the nightingale in the garden of Wentworth House. But this is from a work of fiction.

PAMELA FRANKAU (1908-1967)

Novelist, author of "The Willow Cabin," etc., daughter of Gilbert Frankau, cousin of Diana Raymond. One of her books, "Ask Me No More," is partly set in Hampstead. It was dramatised and presented at the Theatre Royal, Windsor, directed by Margaret Webster with whom P.F. lived at 55, Christchurch Hill, from 1957 until her death.

FICTION—

By the time that she reached Hampstead, she felt soothed and sleepy. Now she came into her kingdom, the house on the leafy corner. There was nothing here to vex the mind or eye. Opening the gate in the wall she found the white façade with the bow windows, the window-boxes full of dwarf tulips. On her left the garden curved away round the corner of the house. On her right, as she crossed the paved yard, there was the leaden cupid from Florence, aiming his fixed arrow. The old clear chime sounded from the church as she put her key in the lock.

from "Ask Me No More," 1958

FACT—

Living in Hampstead is rather like living on a mountain. My local shops cluster above New End Square and when I come out of the dairy I look to my right; the view goes down and down, all the way to the dome of St. Paul's, and beyond. I used, from here, to see the dome silhouetted. I cannot any more. Recently some vast, unwelcome oblong—an office building I assume—has raised itself directly behind the dome, destroying the silhouette.

from an article in "Life," 1966

55, Christchurch Hill

Gardnor Mansions

The Pryors

JOHN HILLABY (1917-)

Travel-writer and journalist, regular walker on the Heath about which he made a TV documentary. Author of "Journey Through Britain", "Journey to the Jade Sea", etc. Has lived in Hampstead since 1952 when, from his home in Tanza Road he led a survey of the Heath.

ANYTHING GOES

This is the Hampstead – the quarter, the village of fashionable fact, the stuff of history books, famous names, buildings, Georgian courts, alleys, narrow streets, once the home of poets, painters and portrait manufacturers, now blocked by traffic, tourists, arty-tarty boutiques, ridiculously expensive antique shops and beautiful resident birds and their boyfriends. A rallying point for hyper-conservatism, Marxism, liberalism and forlorn hopes of all kinds. You can wear anything or do anything. Nobody notices. It's all been done before; it's all been seen before. When a black girl in a topless piece of white chiffon clip-clopped up Haverstock Hill, a newspaper vendor said: 'Y'know if Lady Godiva rode 'ere I bet someone would just pat the nose of 'er 'orse'.

from "Journey Through Love," 1976

165

KATHLEEN FARRELL (1912-)

Novelist and writer of stories for children lived in Hampstead from the beginning of World War Two until 1968 at various addresses in Heath Street and Flask Walk. In 1959 her novel "The Common Touch" had a launching party at the High Hill Bookshop.

COFFEE BARS AND CONVERSATION

.... my 'special' local is *The Coffee Cup in High Street*, which has the only *terrasse chauffée* in Hampstead, where one can sit outside even in winter, warmed by overhead heaters. But why, oh why, can't we have more tables and chairs on that wide wide pavement? This is our *Cafe de la paix*; sit there long enough and all Hampstead will pass by, and many will not pass, but sit somewhere, on wooden stools, or even on the edges of tables, and exchange gossip....

'Now this novel I'm writing', says the man who looks like a Bank Manager, but surely cannot be? 'I'm doing the descriptive bits and my friend is writing in the sex....'

'I know I'm good', says the middle-aged actor, but I can't get anything except these bloody commercials. And trying to light a cigarette on Stonehenge in a sixty mile an hour gale isn't what I'm used to'....

An Austrian doctor of philosophy with an acute - but possibly kindly- eye, looks sharply around for a few seconds, sees all he wants to, which is probably all there is to see, and goes back behind his newspaper.

from "The Heathside Book", 1962

55, Flask Walk →

JOHN MORTIMER (1923-)

Novelist, dramatist, barrister, lived in Harben Road, Swiss Cottage, from the late 1940s until the early 1960s. When "The Book of Hampstead," which heralded a resurgence of native publishing, appeared in 1960, he reviewed it in "The Spectator." The accompanying extract is culled, with his permission, from that notice.

Cartoon by Ron McTrusty

The point of Hampstead, as a situation or a dream, is surely that it exists at the opposite end of the world from Chelsea. The distance between these two ways of life is extreme, polar, and as endless as the journey on the 31 bus. Sooner or later people decide to which of these two worlds they belong. Are they for the lush pastures of Harrods, the Vogue vouchers to the Royal Court, the tapered trousers and authors' sweaters bought at the male boutiques down the King's Road? Or will they settle for the reproduction Cézanne, the spills by the gas fire, the obedient mirth at yet another festival of the Marx Brothers, and the old Penguin edition of Virginia Woolf?

It is probably a painful choice. Living on the foothills of Hampstead, almost in Kilburn, below the cold snows of the culture belt, I don't feel myself greatly involved in this dilemma. But I know just where my Hampstead, the long grey streets full of exiled professors and string quartets, gives way to the bright uplands, where the architects come singing home to their rye bread and goat's milk cheese and where I once heard a mother tell her child that the teddy bear hot water bottle she had just bought it might be called 'Jocasta.'

Of that Hampstead this book seems a symptom rather than an evocation. Published by a local bookshop, and written by an assortment of local residents, it is full of historical chat and small reminiscence. In the main it is written in prose as exciting as a pair of porridge-coloured pottery book-ends, and exhales an atmosphere as cheerful as that of the late Professor Joad playing hockey on a corner of the Heath. Those who like Hampstead will like it very much.

IN LONDON LAST NIGHT

Hampstead is the Parnassus of London's literates. A hundred novelists live within its boundaries.

At a publisher's party there last night a Guy Fawkes of letters could virtually have put an end to English novel-writing.

The party was to celebrate Miss KATHLEEN FARRELL'S book "The Common Touch". She lives in a Hampstead cottage. She writes on the backs of envelopes and laundry lists.

Novelist KAY DICK was there, wearing a monocle. E. ARNOT ROBERTSON disguised herself in a Garbo hat. And there was the man with the Midas touch, Mr. DAVID DIVINE, who achieved what every novelist's bank manager dreams of – his novel, "Boy on a Dolphin", was made into a film.

'We could have screamed at him when he said it was nearly all luck, really."

from "Evening Standard," 4 February, 1959

DRABBLE'S HAMPSTEAD

They came from Frognal and Fitzjohn's Avenue, from Heath Hurst Road and Highgate. In open-necked shirts and corduroy they looked as if they had just fallen out of bed and jogged across the Heath – which, for the most part, they had. Here were Hampstead's literary sons and daughters bound for the shop where Margaret Drabble was throwing a party for her new work, the Oxford Companion to English Literature.

Of course everyone was there: Lady Antonia Fraser talked books to Sir Angus Wilson…. Salman Rushdie to Julian Barnes, Melvyn Bragg to Hunter Davies and Christopher Hampton to Michael Holroyd. Then they all swapped partners and talked books some more.

from "The Standard" 29.4.85

PAUL JENNINGS (1918 –)

Humorous writer, contributed the "Oddly Enough" column to the Observer for many years. Lived at 4, Prospect Place during the 1950s.

ROAD SAFETY ENIGMA

…. it was on the way up to Hampstead Heath last Sunday that I was quite happily jerked back into Britishness. For there, in the window of a sweetshop, was a long card which quite certainly bore, in large capitals, the surrealist legend

ERTGHECEKTATEA

It was irresistible. I stopped to read and found that these were the jumbled letters of a Road Safety slogan. One had to send in the correct solution, together with another, original slogan; there were prizes. Instantly, I was at home, charmed by the calm, kindly amateurishness of the whole thing, inviting a democratic public to play a parlour game to fight a serious social evil. I was back in Hampstead, back from the mad, horn-blowing motorists of the Continent with their absurd white caps; back in Hampstead, where it *always* seems to be Road Safety Week, with posters, for some reason, of seals crossing the road, and an enormous thatched cottage called "Courtesy House" trundling through the streets on a six-wheeled lorry from which come loud-speaker appeals that nobody hears….

from "Even Oddlier" 1952

DONALD OGDEN STEWART (1894-1980)

Film script writer, contributor to "The New Yorker," playwright, victim of McCarthyism, lived at 103 Frognal from 1953 until his death. Ella Winter, his wife, survived him by only two days.

HOLLYWOOD COMES TO HAMPSTEAD

Our agents kept searching, and one of them mentioned a funny old house on a hill in Hampstead which had belonged to Ramsay Macdonald. It had been unoccupied for many years and had become dilapidated. There was dry rot and rising damp, the curtains were moth-eaten, the roof leaked and the garden was an overgrown jungle. The paint was chipped and there was no furniture to speak of. It was in such poor condition that the Macdonald family didn't want to rent it, fearing what they would have to pay to fix it up. We stayed there for a long time without either renting it or buying it. Ella loved the house but the work that had to be done scared us both.

It was Katie Hepburn who came and saved us from our indecision. She is very interested in old houses and when she saw this one she said that it was a beautiful place and why don't we rent it for a year. She came every day for about six weeks with a packed lunch from the Connaught Hotel and helped Ella fix the place up. She took a scythe and hacked away at the grass in the back yard, which was over six feet high. She and Ella would sit on crates in what is now the kitchen and Katie would dab at the chips in the wall....

WITH CAST OF THOUSANDS

.... In addition to serving as a home for us, our pictures, and a constantly changing menagerie of cats, dogs, a monkey and assorted other creatures, our house has been a gathering place for many friends from many countries. Ingrid Bergman always comes to see us when she's in London, as do the Chaplins and Ring Lardner, Jr., Jim and Helen Thurber were here several times before Jim's death, and so were Edmund Wilson and Ella's old friend Robinson Jeffers. We had parties for the Berliner Ensemble and for the Moscow Arts Theater.... Many American friends came to see us after they had escaped the net of the blacklist. One of these was Paul Robeson, who had just had his passport returned by the State Department and was able for the first time in several years to travel out of the U.S.

from "_By a Stroke of Luck_," 1975

EDWARD CARTER (1902-1982)

Architect, spent many years with ASLIB and UNESCO, became director of the Architectural Association in 1961. Lived in Keats Grove until his retirement in the 'seventies.

FLASHERS RULE

In Hampstead the architectural quality of Flask Walk is the same as that of Church Row, albeit for a lower-income group. This is one of the places so coveted by the rich that, by a skilful house-agent manoeuvre, the whole of this delectable terrace was seized from working-class families (some of whom had lived in it for generations) and converted gaudily into luxury 'bijou period residencies'. Locally Flask Walk is now known as Flash Walk.

from "The Future of London," 1962

Photograph by EDWIN SMITH

KAY DICK (1915-)

Author, journalist, lived at various Hampstead addresses from the early 1940s until 1968, including Gardnor House, Flask Walk, which was also the home of novelists Kingsley Amis and Elizabeth Jane Howard during the 1970s

A CAPACIOUS POCKET

Flask Walk is more than a street, especially if one is in love with it as are most of those who know it and live in it and about it. It is a self-contained topographical and human unit. It has the picaresque individuality of a French quartier, because within its almost visible boundaries exists a village apart from the greater, more worldly Hampstead village, which older inhabitants of the Walk call 'the town.'

One comes into Flask Walk and goes out of Flask Walk, which is quite different from passing through or going up and down an ordinary street. We are, as it were, a world within a world, an uneven-shaped oval, scooped out of the smaller Hampstead hills, protected by two naturally narrow axes, leading at one end into the High Street and its traffic, at the other to the crossroads that link us to Well Walk and the Heath. Equally fashioned for independency is the associative area of the Walk, flanked on one side by small alleyways (Back Lane and Luton and Murray Terraces) which serve as tributaries to our main stream. The decisive pattern becomes clearer when correlated with the two curving inclines leading to New End Square and given a finality by the deceptively quiet backwater of Gardnor Road. This curious symmetry is often referred to as 'the pocket', that is the pocket in which the flask is carried and protected.

from "The Heathside Book", 1962

Kay Dick *Pamela Frankau*

MELVYN BRAGG (1939 –)

Novelist, editor and presenter of television features about the arts, regular contributor to "<u>Punch</u>". Resident of Hampstead since 1970. Until 1979 he lived at 9, Gayton Road which in his novel "<u>The Nerve</u>" (1971) is called Tagon Street.

Photo: London Weekend Television Ltd.

[In "*The Nerve*" Bragg's hero, on the verge of a breakdown, emerges from Tagon Street into....

'...that High Street: now I come round the corner of my own street and I am on it: the noise!'

'It was as if my skull enlarged itself, swelled up on my shoulders and laid itself across the road as across an executioner's block. And through it went the lorries full of rubble, grinding gears and whining brakes, the sports cars and motor-bikes, the 268 bus and the dustcart now proceeding on their business in this High Street at the busiest time of the morning: all drove right through that shell of skull.

'On a Sunday morning, without the traffic, Hampstead High Street and Heath Street are lovely: Georgian shops, delicate shades of brick, alleyways full of galleries and antiques, pottery and bright goods: dozens of pubs and restaurants; bookshops and eccentric clothes shops, delicatessens, launderettes, record shops, luxury shops: Victorian frontages – the hangover of a more stolid time – hardware shops, wood shops, old grocery shops and sweet shops, a cobbler, a fish and chip place and the most old-fashioned Woolworths in England; newsagents where they'd take minutes to get you the exact size of brown envelope, fruit shops where they'd rummage for the best apples; builders' merchants up some of those back alleys and, being Hampstead, all sorts of cottage industries in pretty backyards – furniture, mats, health foods, hand-painted posters, ties, shirts – within a few hilly acres was concentrated the variety of a huge city: those two streets were in some measure the quintessence of the West End of London *and* a lively suburb *and* a county town *and* a university area: and the alleys and slits between the walls, the unexpected squares and groups of trees and sudden revelation of Georgian cottages or Victorian strength or Edwardian grace – all this had made Hampstead seem to me to be the centre of everything I wanted from a *place* for a few years. That was when I'd come: and why I'd come.'

MARGARET DRABBLE (1939-)

Novelist, biographer of Arnold Bennett and editor of the "Oxford Companion to English Literature." She has lived in Hampstead since the late 1960s. The accompanying extract comes from "The Middle Ground," published in 1980.

Photograph by ALLAN TITMUSS

It would do us all good to get out, said Kate, so off we went to Hampstead Heath, to Kenwood, pushchairs and wellingtons piled into the back of my car and of Evelyn's, leaving Judith sleeping. We started off with a cursory tour of the house, small boots skidding on the parquet, unsuitable little fingers wiping themselves at knee level on pale paint. Kate was wearing a striped woolly hat with a bobble, and her cheeks were pink with cold and health. 'What a life,' she said, gazing at the Adam library with its bright colours and restored elegance. 'Do you think that if one were a rich person and lived in a house like this one would become a proper person, and live at a proper pace? Slowly, I mean?' We paused in front of my favourite painting, Van Dyck's handsome Duke of Richmond, sitting back with a knowing smile on his fine lips, his red-gold curls tumbling, his white shirt billowing, his faithful dog gazing up at him with an expression of alert fidelity, a spear leaning against his chair with casual potency. Ease, grace, wealth, power; an embroidered curtain, a distant landscape, a red robe. 'Now *there's* a man,' said Evelyn, and Kate agreed. Kate dismissed the famous Vermeer, which was to cause such a sensation when stolen a few years later: plump, dull, pretentiously simple, trying to be the real thing, she said, but not the real thing at all. What do you mean by the real thing, I asked her, and she said, Oh, Peter de Hooch, of course, you know that one in the National Gallery, of the woman and her maid in a back yard with a fish in a bucket and a man coming down the alleyway? That is the most beautiful picture ever painted, she said, with mocking emphasis.....

When we emerged from the house, the swollen dark slate sky had filled with thick white mist. We couldn't even see the lake with its little two-dimensional bridge at the bottom of the landscaped grassy slope. Bare trees loomed suddenly, alarm-ingly. Some of the children wanted to go back, but others wanted to go on, so on we went, past Dr. Johnson's summer house and the high rhododendrons, past a bench with an empty fish tin on it ('That was there last week,' said Evelyn, 'do you think it's the same one?'), through a deep branching alley of evergreen, and out into a strange white plain, all distances vanished, only damp white slopes with rooks pecking at pale tufts of straw-coloured grass, and one ominous magpie. It was silent, eerie, all sound muffled. All other walkers had disapp-eared. We were alone in a sea of mist. Forty rooks, stiff-legged, looked up at us, but did not move away. They were in possession, sinister in their assurance, their indifference to our passing. We walked on, careful to keep all seven children in view.

KINGSLEY AMIS (1922 –)

*Novelist, anthologist, lecturer, also lived
(late-70s, early-80s) at Gardnor House, Flask Walk.*

PROVINCIAL HAMPSTEAD ?

I first lived in Hampstead in the mid-sixties, in Keats Grove, and
for me that part is still the best, prettiest and (yes) most romantic
bit of the place. To the eye, Hampstead is not so much a village as a
smallish country town, fetched perhaps from somewhere in the West
of England and enclosed by suburbia on three sides and grassland
on the fourth.

from Preface to Ann Usborne's "A Portrait of Hampstead," 1984

182

Gardnor House

ALISON LURIE

Contemporary American novelist who lived at 60, Flask Walk from January-June, 1970. She is Professor of English at Cornell University.

THE WEDGE-SHAPED HOUSE

"...we rented this house by mail; the agent sent us a photograph and description. The morning we got here, off the plane, Flask Walk was so pretty: the sun was shining for once, and when the taxi stopped it looked just like the picture, only better because it was in color, a perfect Georgian cottage. And I thought well, damn it, it's really worth all that rent and plane fare and those eight hellish hours with Jakie on the plane. And then we went inside, and the back of the house wasn't there, like it had been sliced off. Of course the real estate agent hadn't said anything about that." The Vogeler's house is on a sharp-angled corner; it consists of a basement kitchen, a sitting room, and two bedrooms, one above the other. Each room is narrowly triangular; the shape of a piece of pie cut far less generously than Debby has just served....

Turning off the High Street, Fred plunges into Hampstead Tube Station, buys a ticket to Notting Hill Gate, and enters an ancient iron lift decorated with advertising posters of half-naked young women. As it descends into the cold damp shaft, so he descends against his will, into naked memories.

from "Foreign Affairs," 1984

184

ALAN COREN (1938 –)

Journalist, author of many volumes of humourous writing, editor of "Punch" since 1978. Rector of St. Andrew's University, 1973-6. To indicate "Punch's awareness of the Millennium he devoted two pages to it in the first issue for 1986. Has lived in Swiss Cottage, now lives in Cricklewood (just over the border from NW3).

MILLENNIAL MILESTONES

986 Monks of Westminster granted Manor of Hampstead. Nuns of Westminster demand name be changed to Personor of Hampstead, set up Ad Hoc Sisterhood Consciousness Protest Solidarity Committee, burn wimples, learn judo. Hampstead Battered Nun Refuge founded by Sister Erin, Mother Vastly Superior. ....

1067 England's first *Cuisine Normande* restaurant opened in Heath Street. Adrian the Svelte does the cooking and his friend Pippin the Trick waits on tables. Speciality: mince. ....

1215 King John signs MAGNA CARTA, in High Hille Bokeshop. Last-minute clause inserted by barons gives them 15% on all sales over first ten thousand, plus 50% of vellumback rights.

1290 Expulsion of Jews by Edward I. Collapse of Hampstead house prices.

1349 Black Death strikes England, bringing grief, terror, misery, and, in Hampstead, extreme annoyance. Residents refuse to pay rates until local health authority agrees to drop the word *black*. ....

1476 Caxton sets up first printing press. 93% of Hampstead population send him manuscript novels about marital disharmony. ....

1616 Death of Shakespeare. "OVER-RATED"– *Hampstead & Highgate Expresse*. ....

1750 Death of J. S. Bach, giving whole of Hampstead wonderful opportunity to point out he was not a patch on W.F. Bach, K.P.E. Bach, J.C.B. Bach, or, indeed, Sugar Ray Bach, the Leipzig cruiserweight. ....

1938 Freud leaves Vienna, arrives in Hampstead. Woken on first morning by 34,000 local patients queueing in road outside. ....

Burgh House, venue of literary events

INDEX TO OBSERVERS:

190

GRATEFUL ACKNOWLEDGEMENTS TO THE UNDERMENTIONED FOR PERMISSION . . . . TO QUOTE FROM

A. Alvarez and the proprietors of Esquire	Why I Live where I Live
Kingsley Amis & Damien Tunnacliffe	Portrait of Hampstead
Melvyn Bragg & Secker & Warburg Ltd.	The Nerve
The Executors of the late Ivor Brown & IPC	London (Newnes, 1960)
John Carswell & Secker & Warburg Ltd.	Lying Awake by Catherine Carswell
Penguin Books	The Future of London by Edward Carter
John Grey Murray & John Murray (Publishers) Ltd.	The Other Half by Kenneth Clark
Lettice Cooper & Victor Gollancz Ltd.	Black Bethlehem
Alan Coren & The Proprietors of Punch	Millennial Milestones
Hunter Davies & Hamish Hamilton Ltd.	A Walk Round London's Parks
Kay Dick	The Pocket of Flask Walk
Margaret Drabble & Weidenfeld & Nicolson Ltd.	The Middle Ground
Dame Daphne du Maurier & Victor Gollancz Ltd.	Growing Pains
J. M. Dent Ltd.	Preface to Trilby
Kathleen Farrell	Coffee Bars and Conversation
The executors of Eleanor Farjeon	No. 23 The High
The Editor & Proprietors of the Ham & High	Hymn for Hampstead by Michael Foot
Edward Arnold Ltd. & Penguin Books Ltd.	A Passage to India by E. M. Forster
A. P. Watt Ltd.	Ask Me No More by Pamela Frankau
"	The Golden Echo by David Garnett
Maire Gaster	The unpublished autobiography of Sylvia Lynd, Essays of Robert Lynd, the poem Wistaria by Sylvia Lynd and the introduction to the autobiography. The poems and the essays were published by Dent.
Livia Gollancz & Victor Gollancz Ltd.	Reminiscences of Affection by Victor Gollancz
Chatto & Windus Ltd.	Recollections by Geoffrey Grigson
Macmillan Publishers Ltd.	A House in Hampstead by Thomas Hardy
John Hillaby & Constable & Co. Ltd.	Journey Through Love
Michael Holroyd	Notes on George Bernard Shaw
C. W. Ikin	Hampstead Heath
Simon Jenkins & Collins, Publishers	The Companion Guide to Outer London
Paul Jennings, Max Reinhardt & The Observer	Even Oddlier
The Executors of C. E. M. Joad	The Book of Joad published by Faber & Faber
William Heinemann Ltd.	The Last Laugh by D. H. Lawrence
David Cornwell, Hodder & Stoughton Ltd. & Pan Books	Smiley's People by John Le Carre
Jeanne & Norman Mackenzie & Weidenfeld & Nicolson Ltd.	The Time Traveller

Mrs. J. Nairn. . . . . Nairn's London by Ian Nairn
The Executors of George Orwell, Secker & Warburg
       and Penguin Books Ltd. . . . . Keep the Aspidistra Flying
Dieter Pevsner & Penguin Books Ltd. . . . . . The Buildings of England by Nikolaus Pevsner
Sir David Piper & Collins, Publishers . . . . The Companion Guide to London
The Executors of Arthur Ransome & Jonathan Cape Ltd. Autobiography by Arthur Ransome
Diana Raymond & A. P. Watt Ltd. . . . . Strangers' Gallery by Diana Raymond &
       An Old Platoon by Ernest Raymond
The Executors of J. B. Priestley &
       William Heinemann Ltd. . . . . . . Margin Released
John Richardson & Historical Publications Ltd. . Hampstead 1000
Alastair Service. . . . . A Walk Through Victorian & Edwardian
       Hampstead
Sir Stephen Spender & Faber & Faber Ltd. . . . . . World Within World
The Executors of Donald Ogden Stewart . . . . By a Stroke of Luck
J. C. Trewin. . . . . Down to the Lion and
       The Heath they say is Hampstead
Wendy Trewin. . . . . Diaries in Down to the Lion
Professor F. M. L. Thompson. . . . . Hampstead : The Building of a Borough
Rayner Unwin and Unwin Hyman Ltd. . . . . . . The Truth about a Publisher
       by Sir Stanley Unwin
Peter Vansittart & Quartet Books . . . . Paths from a White Horse
Christopher Wade. . . . . The Streets of Hampstead
The Executors of Beatrice Webb & Virago Books . . . The Diaries of B. Webb
A. P. Watt Ltd. . . . . Experiment in Autobiography by H. G. Wells
Chatto & Windus Ltd. . . . . The Man with a Hammer by Anna Wickham
The Executors of Clough Williams-Ellis . . . . . Architect Errant
The Executors of Leonard Woolf & The Hogarth Press . Diaries of Virginia Woolf
The Executors of Edwin Muir. . . . . Autobiography by Edwin Muir
The Executors of John Middleton Murry . . . . Between Two Worlds
Professor Latham & Unwin Hyman Ltd. . . . . . . The Diaries of Samuel Pepys in the
       definitive edition first published by
       Bell & Hyman Ltd.

Grateful acknowledgement also to JOHN CARSWELL for his suggestions for what was
included in the exhibition on which this book is based, and for permission to use the
photograph of his mother, Catherine Carswell; to the Trustees of the National Portrait
Gallery for permission to reproduce portraits of Arnold Bennett, Wilkie Collins,
Daniel Defoe, Charles Dickens, Michael Drayton, John Evelyn, E. M. Forster, Leigh Hunt,
Samuel Johnson, John Keats, D. H. Lawrence, Samuel Pepys, J. B. Priestley, John Ruskin,
Bernard Shaw, Stephen Spender, H. G. Wells and Virginia Woolf. And to Olive Cook for
permission to use the photograph of Edward Carter by her late husband, Edwin Smith, and
to the other photographers named in the text.